THE SECOND GREAT CRASH

Frances Cairncross
& Hamish McRae

PRENTICE-HALL, INC.
Englewood Cliffs, New Jersey

The Second Great Crash, by Frances Cairncross and Hamish McRae

First published in Great Britain by Eyre Methuen, Ltd.
First American Edition published by Prentice-Hall, Inc., 1975

Printed in the United States of America

10 9 8 7 6 5 4 3 2 1

Library of Congress Cataloging in Publication Data

Cairncross, Frances.
The second great crash.

1. Economic history—1945- 2. Inflation
(Finance) I. McRae, Hamish, joint author.
II. Title.
HC59.C253 1975 330.9'047 75-5740
ISBN 0-13-797530-9

CONTENTS

FRANCES CAIRNCROSS joined the Business News staff of *The Times* in 1967. She worked briefly for *The Banker* in 1969 and later for *The Observer*. Now she broadcasts regularly on BBC radio and is economics correspondent of *The Guardian*.

HAMISH McRAE was assistant and then deputy editor of *The Banker* until 1972, when he went to *Euromoney* as editor. He has since also joined *The Guardian* and is their newly-appointed financial editor.

The authors married in 1971. This is the second book that they have written together. The first (*Capital City*) was published by Eyre Methuen in 1973 and quickly had a second edition in paperback.

What This Book Is About

This book is the story of the breakdown of the world's economic system. In one sense the Second Great Crash has already happened. When the book was begun, in late 1974, most major stock markets had already fallen by more than they did in the original Great Crash of 1929.

This collapse of the stock markets, dramatic though it looked, affected the lives of ordinary people much less than the acceleration of inflation. In the first half of 1974, in the seven biggest industrial countries, consumer prices were on average 15 percent higher than in the second half of 1973—which in turn had seen inflation already well into double figures. In one country, Japan, prices were a hair-raising 30 percent up in the last half of 1973.

It was generally believed that by early 1975 prices would be rising more slowly. Hyperinflation—the days of "wheelbarrow wages"—would be postponed. But the reason for expecting inflation to slow down promised another peril in 1975. It was the imminent threat of world slump.

Between the first half of 1973 and the first half of 1974 the world's economic growth skidded to a halt. In the first half of 1973, real output in the industrial world's seven biggest countries was growing at an annual rate of 8½ percent. In the first half of 1974 it *fell* at an annual rate of about 2 percent. How far it would recover in the twelve months following was very hard to see.

The dangers ahead were summed up by the Organization for Economic Cooperation and Development in its July 1974 *Economic Outlook*. "If world demand grows more strongly than foreseen," said the OECD lugubriously, "there will be little chance of reducing the extremely high rate of inflation; if, on the other hand, demand grows less than foreseen, there is a danger of a recession which would no doubt have an impact on inflation but which might soon lead to an excessive reversal of policy, thus preparing the way for a new burst of inflation later." Either way we lose.

The situation has been complicated by the rise in the oil price. It has accentuated all the alarming tendencies that were already apparent. It has added to inflation, increased the danger of world slump, and put a new strain on the already shaky international financial system.

You have no doubt been reading for years about international currency crises, about balance of payments deficits, about the gyrations of economic policy. You must often have felt, understandably, that none of it had much to do with your own standard of living. What is happening now is different. In the past, despite these abstract threats most people got richer. By the time you read this, you will almost certainly be *worse* off than you were back in the autumn of 1973. One of the aims of this book is to explain why.

It may be that, this time round, we shall escape a return to something like the dark years of the 1930s. But if we escape this time, then we have only gained a breathing-space. Either uncontrollable inflation and/or unfathomable slump will catch up with us later in the 1970s.

That much is certain.

1

The Deteriorating World Economy

When the going was good

It always helps to be able to blame one's troubles on somebody else, particularly if that somebody is foreign and rich. The Arabs, by suddenly raising the price of oil, have offered themselves as ready-made culprits of world economic disorder. But the truth is that theirs is only a share—and a tiny share—of the blame for the current alarming combination of inflation and slump. Indeed we have to thank the Arabs and other primary producers for having underwritten the Western world's prosperity in the years following the Second World War.

Looked back upon, the post-war years were something of a golden age. They were the years characterized by the United Kingdom's prime minister Harold Macmillan's famous (if misquoted) phrase of the 1959 election: "You've never had it so good." This was a period when the world seemed to have stumbled on a magic formula for ensuring faster growth than ever known before, coupled with full and stable employment and a rate of inflation which, if fast by 19th century standards, looks trivial by today's.

We are still too close to those golden years to know just why they were such a remarkable period of prosperity. At the time, economists used to attribute it to the skills of economic management, industrialists to advances of efficiency in their factories, bankers to their wisdom in managing money. It is still impossible to be sure. But it does seem that the post-war prosperity ultimately came to be sustainable only at a cost. That cost was inflation.

At first, in the period of recovery from the war, the prosperity was understandable enough. Three factors go a long way to explain it. One was the dismantling of restrictions on international trade and capital movements which had grown up in the 1930s and survived the war. By the end of the 1950s, most European countries' currencies had once again become convertible for external holders into U.S. dollars. Multinational negotiations pulled down trade barriers, the high point of the post-war drive to free trade coming with the Kennedy Round of the mid-1960s. Increasingly, money and goods could move freely from one country to another.

The second factor was the increase in the size of the industrial labor force. In most European countries and in Japan, the agricultural revolution which Britain had seen in the 19th century had hardly begun to take place when the Second World War broke out. Millions of workers were still employed on peasant small-holdings. As they moved into the towns and found jobs in industry, their productivity increased enormously. For some countries, such as Italy and America, there was also a big regional shift of population, with workers from the Italian Mezzogiorno flocking to Turin and Milan, and black workers from Mississippi and Arkansas pouring into southern towns like Atlanta and northern industrial cities like Detroit and Chicago to look for work. In other countries there was an influx of immigrants—Algerians into France, Indians and West Indians into Britain, Turks and Yugoslavs into Germany—to increase the population of working age. These were the days when the social problems caused by rapid shifts in population were only beginning to be perceived. No less important than these movements of population was the rise in the numbers of women going to work. The habit of women working had been encouraged by the war. Now, the widespread use of contraception made family planning easier, people began to have their children earlier, while at the same time the average age of marriage fell steadily. Thus a growing number of women all over the industrial world found themselves, in their early thirties, with their children at school and the time to go out to work.

Finally there was the advent of full employment itself. The politicians who ran the post-war world, and their civil servants, had spent their formative years in the horrors of the Great Depression. For them, unemployment was the ultimate evil—just as the trade cycle had been for their 19th century predecessors. All over the industrial world full employment became the first priority of post-war governments. In the United States in the mid-1960s it even seemed possible to give everybody a higher standard of living, carry out ambitious social programs at home and abroad, send men to the moon and fight a major war all at the same time—and all this without overstraining the economy. With almost every able-bodied man in work, it was hardly surprising if the post-war world achieved rates of growth which looked dramatic compared with anything before 1939.

Everywhere the magic formula seemed to work. The world seemed to be able to achieve faster growth than ever before, and the main question in most people's minds was how to make growth faster still. But other people were underwriting the prosperity of the West. Perhaps those who contributed most were the primary producers, the developing countries who supplied the Western world with raw materials. From their Korean war peak until the commodity price explosion in the early 1970s, the prices of primary products relative to manufactured goods fell steadily. In the first ten of these twenty years, they fell in absolute terms too. In other words, Western industrial countries were able to pay their workers more, to build their factories and to sell their consumer goods, while all the time buying cheaper food, metals and basic commodities largely from countries poorer than themselves.

Above all, the West bought cheaper oil. The price of oil fell through the 1960s even relative to other raw materials. In the 1960s the export price of Saudi Arabian oil in U.S. dollars fell slightly, in sharp contrast to the price of everything else.

It was not until 1972 that the West was to begin, quite suddenly, to suffer for the years of dependence on cheap raw materials and cheap oil. Long before that, however, another cost had made itself felt: inflation.

The price of prosperity

Economists differ, as they invariably do over questions that really matter, on the causes of the acceleration of inflation towards the end of the 1960s. The next chapter looks at the view that the U.S. balance of payments deficit in the 1960s was at the root of the trouble. But the monetarists' view of the world is probably only part of the story. Another part of the explanation for inflation must lie in the firm commitment to full employment undertaken by post-war governments, most of whose members had grown up in the days of the Depression. As time went on, and as workers who had lived through the horrors of the 1930s grew old, the pledge to full employment became increasingly difficult to combine with the rising expectations of the labor force that was beginning to replace them.

After the war, the workers of the Western industrial countries had quickly become accustomed to the idea that every year would see an improvement in their living standards. This improvement might take the form of a bigger car or it might be a shorter line in the doctor's waiting room. It might represent either more private consumption or more public spending. People wanted both. With time, it became harder and harder for the system to deliver growth without inflation.

It became harder partly because the mainsprings of rapid growth immediately after the war began to run down. There were fewer barriers to trade and capital movements to dismantle. There was a slower growth in the work force, as the move from the land tailed off and as countries became more nervous about allowing ever-larger inflows of immigrants before the last lot had been properly absorbed.

But as the work force grew more slowly, the burden which it had to sustain increased. Before the war, primary-school education had been general in most industrial countries. Now secondary-school education became general—and higher education became increasingly common. That meant a better educated work force—but paying for improved education took scarce resources, either public or private, and while young people were at school or college they were not in productive employment.

At the other end of the age scale, too, the burden was getting heavier. Advances in medicine meant that the proportion of old people in the population increased in all industrial countries. Social changes meant that fewer old people were looked after by their families at home. Old people were expensive to care for—and the very old, the over-75s whose numbers were growing fastest, were of all the most expensive to look after properly. At the same time the age of retirement was creeping down. Again, as the work force everywhere in the industrial world began to grow more slowly, it had to support the increasing cost of caring for the old.

To some extent rises in productivity helped to make it possible for growth to continue at rapid rates. But by the late 1960s in all industrial countries there was a noticeable shift of people and jobs out of industry and into the service sector—offices, tourism, and above all the social services. The rising demand for education and for health services which the growth in the numbers of students and retired people created meant at the same time a larger proportion of the work force employed in providing these services. In all these jobs, advances in productivity came slowly. It is easy, by investing in new machinery, to increase the value of the daily output of a man on a factory line. But how do you increase the efficiency of a clerk in a government department or the output of a school teacher?

So a more slowly growing work force was having to generate the resources to meet constantly rising expectations. Not surprisingly, the work force put a higher and higher value on its services. Workers asked for more money—and usually they got it, even when governments had preempted most of the extra resources available to keep public services going.

Why did countries not stamp out inflation in the 1960s, when it was still in single figures? There are two answers to this, and both are partly true. One is that governments felt increasingly unsure of their ability to get rid of inflation. The other was that they doubted their electorates' willingness to pay the price.

Most governments in the 1960s sought to reconcile full employment with stable prices. To European governments prices and incomes policy often seemed to offer the key. Usually, a government would begin with a freeze, which would be effective for a few months. Then the freeze would produce shortages and anomalies—goods would disappear, skilled workers would be harder to find—and the freeze would turn into some kind of period of severe restraint. Finally, the severe restraint would peter out into milder restraint—and eventually there would be a burst of "catching-up" inflation, after which it would be difficult to argue that the trend rate of inflation had been affected at all.

When prices and incomes policies broke down, governments tended to resort to the harsher measure of deflation. Unemployment would rise and prices would accelerate more slowly. But through the 1960s, each time governments tried this technique the rate of inflation seemed to slow down a little less, and it apparently took a higher level of unemployment to produce any measureable effect. This was in any case a remedy which governments were hesitant about using. Not only were they anxious, for political if not for social reasons, to preserve full employment; it was also easier for electorates to appreciate the evil of unemployment than the evil of inflation.

Inflation, after all, does not involve much waste of real resources. It does not produce bread lines—its statistics do not have a human, photographable face. It works by redistributing income and wealth in an apparently random way. That is the trouble: Such redistribution runs quite counter to the Puritan ethic. The thrifty suffer, as their savings are eroded; the profligate gain, as their debts are wiped out.

In the early 1960s inflation probably contributed to prosperity. It took money from the cautious saver, from those who had reached the end of a working life—and gave it to the risk-taker and to the working man. But as it accelerated, the amounts of money shuffled unseen by rising prices rose faster. One study in America in 1974 calculated that the total amount of money transferred from savers to borrowers by inflation since the Second World War was a staggering $400,000 million.

Governments were still not sure what price it was worth paying to try to end inflation. They became even less sure after the events of 1969–70. Then, almost all industrial countries suffered a "wages explosion." It was characterized by an increase in labor unrest—such as the aftermath of the "events of May" in France and the waves of strikes in Italy. There was an abrupt jump in wages. Suddenly, many countries found the old relationship between wage rises and unemployment breaking down.

Unemployment in many countries rose sharply in 1970–1. The familiar remedy of deflation was used once more all over the industrial world. But everywhere it took longer to work and seemed to have less impact than in the past. Countries were left confused and uncertain. They began to doubt whether there was any effective cure for inflation at all.

Into step on stop-go

We might, for all this, have survived for some time with gradually accelerating inflation. But what finally precipitated the present crisis was that in their attempts to squash the inflation of 1969–70 almost all the industrial countries found themselves deflating at the same time. The trade cycle, which plagued the 19th-century world and convinced Karl Marx that the days of capitalist society were numbered, suddenly seemed to return.

Thus 1971 saw slow growth and rising unemployment in all the major industrial countries. Of the seven biggest OECD countries, only Canada grew faster than it had done on average in the 1960s. In 1972 most countries were taking energetic steps to reflate. In 1973, in the seven biggest industrial countries, only Italy and Japan grew *slower* than they had done on

Growth of real GNP in seven major OECD countries: percentage changes

	Average 1959–60 to 1970–1	*1971*	*1972*	*1973*	*1974**
Canada	4.9	5.5	5.8	6.8	4½
U.S.A.	3.9	2.7	6.1	5.9	–1¾
Japan	11.1	6.7	9.4	10.2	–3¼
France	5.8	5.1	5.5	6.0	4¾
Germany	4.9	2.8	3.0	5.3	1
Italy	5.5	1.1	3.4	6.0	4¾
U.K.	2.9	1.4	3.5	5.3	–½
Total	5.3	3.3	5.8	6.5	–¼

Source: OECD *Economic Outlook*, variously
* Forecast from December 1974 *Economic Outlook*

average in the 1960s. After the boom was over, the OECD in its *Economic Outlook* of December 1973 saw things this way: "The strength of the upswing since the end of 1971 and the coincidence of its timing among practically all member countries has been unprecedented. The generalized nature and extent of the expansion has probably contributed to the early and widespread development of capacity bottlenecks in many basic industries—a situation in which countries could find only limited relief through imports."

Between 1971 and 1973, world output rose by a staggering 17 percent. Bottlenecks quickly appeared. In the U.S.A., for instance, the Federal Reserve index of capacity utilization in such major materials industries as basic metals, textiles, and paper and pulp was already by the middle of 1973 at the highest level it had ever shown.

As the industrial world had swung into step on stop-go, a disturbing number of countries reported that it took longer than usual, when they began to reflate, for unemployment to start to fall. Even at the height of the boom, unemployment in many cases was still high in relation to other indicators of slack in the economy. Now, the boom over, an even larger number of countries found that as they reflated, costs and prices began to accelerate sooner and faster than was normally their experience. In the three months to October 1973, the last three months before the oil price increase, inflation in the whole OECD area, seasonally adjusted, was already into double figures, running at an annual rate of 11 percent. For on top of the inflationary forces which the industrial countries had developed within themselves, there appeared a new phenomenon. Commodity prices, which had hardly risen at all during the previous twenty years, now soared at rates which made rises in the prices of industrial goods look trivial.

The commodity boom

If it had been just the capacity of the West's factories and labor force that the growth of the world economy overstretched, inflation would have been given a new fillip. Shortages of manufactured goods and labor would have been enough to cause prices of those goods and wage-rates to move sharply upwards as people and companies bid against each other for these scarce resources. But of itself this would not have caused the price explosion of 1973–4. The trigger for that was commodity price rises: The 1973 boom had overtaxed not only the resources of the industrial world but also, and more particularly, the resources of the primary producers.

Trade in primary products is different from trade in manufactured goods in that it is difficult to increase output suddenly. If a factory gets an order from a new customer, it can usually find extra capacity somewhere. It can plan an extra shift, persuade its workers to put in more overtime, find new machinery or another factory within the group which can take the job, reduce its manning schedules, drop its quality control, or cajole its other customers into accepting slightly later delivery dates.

In other words, the supply of industrial products is elastic. The supply of most primary products is not. There is no way of increasing an annual crop of wheat for twelve months; no way of increasing the coffee crop for several years; and it is difficult to raise the output of minerals suddenly if the mines are already running at capacity.

The result of this was that while the expansion "in step" of the world economy caused the prices of industrial goods to climb, it caused the prices of commodities to rocket. True, the expansion was not the only cause. There were some special factors at work as well, such as the failure of the Russian wheat harvest in 1971 that induced America to sell off much of its surplus stocks of wheat, the floods in Pakistan which destroyed a large part of the 1973 cotton crop, or the strikes in North America and power cuts in Japan which reduced the output of zinc. Sheer speculation almost certainly contributed. Thanks to the huge expansion in the world's money supply in the preceding years, there was plenty of cash around to invest in stockpiling commodities. Distrust of floating exchange rates and depreciating paper money provided a powerful incentive.

But even allowing for special factors, one may single out the astonishing burst of international growth in 1972 and 1973—the fastest the world has ever known—as the most important explanation of the commodity-price explosion.

Explosion it was. At the end of 1971, market prices in sterling for staple commodities other than oil (as measured by the *Economist* Commodity Price Indicator) were between three and four times as high as in 1939. By the spring of 1974 they had trebled again.

The rise was uneven. Some products climbed only gradually, some soared. Thus in mid-1974 beef and coffee were only 50 percent higher in price than they had been in 1970, while sugar and zinc were at roughly seven times their 1970 level. Copper, lead, and tin were all between two and three times the 1970 average, cotton and rubber roughly double, and wool and cocoa three times their 1970 price level.

Most of these rises were packed into eighteen wild months between the autumn of 1972 and the spring of 1974. Over the entire preceding century the total rise had been only twice as great as in that brief period. For most European countries and for Japan, this was a disaster. They are heavy importers of raw materials and commodities, and export mainly manufactured goods. The rise in import prices meant that they were suddenly much worse off. To take the unit values of British imports and exports as a rough and dramatic guide, relative prices moved about 22 percent in favor of British exports over the period from 1953–5 to the autumn of 1972, and 27 percent against British exports over the next year and a half.

This shift in the terms of trade had to be paid for

somehow. Somehow there had to be a shift of resources from the countries of the industrial world to the commodity producers. Often the producers and the industrial countries were one and the same—the U.S.A., Canada and Australia are all both major industrial nations and substantial producers of raw materials. But for those countries that are principally industrial producers and have to rely on imports of raw materials, this shift in the terms of trade meant that they have had to produce more to buy less: In other words, to reduce their standard of living.

Thus by the time the oil producers chose to jack up their prices the Western world had already dug itself in a hole. Its world had got steadily richer, year in, year out, for more than twenty years. Now it had to accept that it was not going to get richer for a while, or at any rate not as quickly as in the past . . . though in the autumn of 1973 it had not yet dared to break the news to its citizens. There was, anyway, a new blow awaiting it: the end to cheap oil.

2

Monetary Order and Disorder

While Bretton Woods worked

The higher price of oil was to hit a world in which inflation was already becoming uncontrollable. Long before that blow fell, there had been signs of strain. They showed in the collapse of the international money system set up at the end of the war at a conference in the small New Hampshire town of Bretton Woods. The system did not break down suddenly. It disintegrated as central bankers and finance ministers fought a long rearguard action to prop it up. Ironically their rescue efforts probably added to the very strains which caused the collapse.

The new monetary order devised at Bretton Woods in 1944 was planned by men who knew only too well how far the economic chaos of the 1930s had been responsible for the holocaust of the war, and how much of the havoc could have been avoided if individual nations had not followed incompatible economic policies. Faced with declining production and employment, each country had tried to increase its own exports and cut back its imports, ignoring the fact that it could only hope to export more if other countries were prepared to import more. Individual prudence meant collective stupidity.

So Bretton Woods planned to outlaw some of the more self-defeating devices employed in the 1930s —such as competitive devaluations—and to try to make sure that countries would not have to fall back on them. The conference led to the formation of the twin institutions, the International Bank for Reconstruction and Development (grandly known as the World Bank) and the International Monetary Fund (IMF). The first was to lend long-term to countries to aid post-war reconstruction, and then to help finance economic development in the Third World; the second was to arbitrate in the new monetary order, to try to discourage countries from resorting to the anti-social "beggar-my-neighbor" tactics of the 1930s, and to lend to countries with short-term balance of payments difficulties.

To rule out competitive devaluations, this new system provided for exchange rates which were fixed against each other, moving up or down only occasionally in formal devaluations or revaluations which required the blessing of the IMF. To stop the proliferation of special currency arrangements and multiple-tier exchange rates which had strangled trade in the 1930s, it insisted that currencies should become fully convertible as soon as possible. That meant that anyone—or at least any central bank—which held (say) Deutschmarks or sterling should be able to present them to the German Bundesbank or to the Bank of England and get them exchanged for other currencies. In the case of dollars, it meant the ultimate right to have them converted by the U.S. Federal Reserve into gold.

For more than a decade this monetary system showed every sign of working splendidly. From 1945 to the end of the 1950s there was an almost uninterrupted move towards free convertibility. True, there were a few false starts—sterling was prematurely declared convertible before the post-war recovery had really got under way. But by the end of the 1950s most European currencies were, for the first time since the 1920s, freely convertible for external holders.

Fixed exchange rates also seemed to work well. Sterling's devaluation in 1949 had produced a general rearrangement of exchange rates; under the Fourth Republic the French had devalued the franc every two or three years; in 1961 the Germans had revalued the mark. But from the late 1950s, exchange-rate changes were rare among the countries of the industrial world. The rock on which Bretton Woods was founded was the almighty U.S. dollar. America's economy had been virtually unscathed by the ravages of the war, and America took the lead in ordering the post-war recovery in the rest of the world. The dollar's exchange rate with gold, at $35 an ounce, had remained unchanged since 1934, one fixed point in a moving world. With the dollar convertible into gold on request and America's gold reserves by far and away the largest in the world, everyone was prepared to accept a dollar "as good as gold."

That was just as well. For there was one problem which Bretton Woods had failed to solve. No arrangements had been made for making sure that the supply of world money increased or for regulating the rate at which it grew. For a long time this did not matter. Throughout the 1950s and 1960s, the U.S. balance of payments was in almost continuous deficit. The dollars which paid for this deficit provided the world with an increasing supply of world money. Eked out with gold and with sterling (the other main reserve currency, which was convertible into dollars), the U.S. dollar financed post-war recovery and economic growth.

For years the international money system worked well. It allowed the world to recover from history's most destructive war in little more than ten years, and without the miseries of the twenties and thirties. But it depended, to an uncomfortable extent, on a strong dollar and on inflexible exchange rates. By the end of the 1960s it had outlived its usefulness.

Almighty no more

The success of the post-war international monetary system depended heavily on the U.S. balance of payments deficit. America's deficit was a reflection partly on the size of her military expenditure overseas: on keeping troops in Europe and, eventually, on fighting in Vietnam. It reflected, too, the steady stream of American investment into other countries' industry. This investment played an important part in helping to finance the recovery and growth of Western Europe and Japan. But it became increasingly resented, particularly in France, and one of the Common Market's early aims was to build up a European industry which would be able to hold its own against America's multinationals.

Above all, the American deficit provided the world with money—with its main sources of new international liquidity. It plugged the gap in the Bretton Woods system. The supply of new gold would have been quite inadequate to finance the growth of post-war trade; the exchange rate between gold and the dollar made mining gold increasingly uneconomic. That left the reserve currencies. But by an unfortunate paradox, running a balance of payments deficit was also the best way of undermining confidence in a currency and so making it unfit to be a reserve currency.

For a while this did not affect the strength of the dollar. People were prepared to hold dollars because of the might of the American economy and of the size of her gold reserves. In the 1950s, governments were content to hold dollars in their reserves. But as the 1960s progressed and America showed no signs of eliminating her deficit, they began to sell their dollars for gold. (The French took this a stage further. Instead of merely asking the American authorities to put their gold in a safe deposit in the vaults of the New York Federal Reserve Bank, they insisted on having their gold shipped across the Atlantic to France.)

Gradually the U.S.A. was forced away from free convertibility. Central banks were quietly persuaded to stop presenting dollars to be exchanged for gold. But the American deficit persisted and grew. Finally in 1971 the balance of trade, which in the past had generally been in surplus, began to slip into deficit. By then it was abundantly clear that the U.S. dollar was overvalued against the other main currencies.

The exchange rates float

Yet the devaluation of the dollar was a long time in coming. The Bretton Woods conference had provided machinery for such countries as wanted to devalue or revalue to do so. But after the long years in which exchange rates had been relatively stable, governments found it harder to accept the need for rates to move.

The belief slowly grew that exchange rates had become stabilized. In the early 1960s the Common Market began to build up its Common Agricultural Policy on the assumption that it had beaten the problem of exchange-rate changes for good, and started to plan for a monetary union which would culminate in the ultimate in fixed exchange rates—a common currency for the members of the EEC.

From believing that exchange rates *would* not change it was a small step to believing that they *should* not. By the time sterling began to come under pressure to devalue, in the mid-1960s, the exchange rate had become a sort of national virility symbol. To allow it to change, and particularly to allow it to be devalued, was a mark of economic impotence.

But if exchange rates had become harder to change, the pressures on them to alter had not vanished. If anything, they increased. There was still inflation, and it still affected different countries in different ways. In some countries, such as Japan, wages rose rapidly, but as productivity was also growing by leaps and bounds, labor costs per unit of output rose relatively slowly. In other countries, such as Britain, big increases in wages were only matched by a sluggish rise in productivity and unit labor costs soared upwards. In some countries, such as Germany, export prices tended to lag behind the price increases for domestic goods. Elsewhere they kept pace.

As the competitiveness of different countries changed, pressures on exchange rates built up. The weakest link in the chain was the U.K., running a growing balance of payments deficit. In 1964 the British General Election was won by Labour. Foreign holders of sterling promptly panicked and sold; and from then on, until the pound was finally devalued in November 1967, there was an almost continuous rescue operation. The IMF and the other central banks lent foreign exchange—mainly dollars—to the Bank of England, to help defend the pound. Between 1964 and 1968 Britain managed to borrow some $8,000 millions—nearly three times as much as its official reserves in 1964.

With the devaluation of sterling, the world of fixed exchange rates began to crumble. By 1971 several major currencies had changed their rates against the U.S. dollar—and the weight of the movement had been downwards. The dollar, in short, had been revalued against other currencies, at a time when it was increasingly clear that it needed to be devalued.

One reason why its devaluation took so long to achieve was that the dollar had become the center of the international monetary system, the standard of value against which other exchange rates were set. It was widely believed that it was simply not possible for the dollar to be devalued—that it was only possible for other currencies to be revalued against it. But the overvalued dollar made it possible for other countries to run balance of payments surpluses. When it came to the crunch, they found they rather liked things that way.

Finally in August 1971 President Nixon forced the hands of other industrial countries by simply declaring the dollar inconvertible. The U.S. Federal Reserve now formally withdrew its promise to exchange dollar bills held by foreign central banks for gold or other currencies. The dollar floated . . . down.

Faced with a choice between holding more dollars of uncertain value and letting their exchange rates rise against the dollar, the industrial countries began to negotiate a new regime of exchange rates, built round a devalued dollar. The outcome—the result of a whole autumn of tough bargaining—was the Smithsonian Agreement reached in Washington, D.C., in December 1971, and described by a triumphant Nixon as "the greatest monetary agreement in the history of the world."

It lasted six months. This attempt to return to the world of the 1950s and 1960s, to the era of fixed exchange rates, began to collapse the following June, when a tidal wave of speculation engulfed sterling and forced the British authorities to let the pound float "as a temporary measure."

For a while the currencies of some of the Common Market countries clung together in a "floating snake," pegged to each other but bobbing together against other currencies. A series of German revaluations kept the snake from bursting. But in spring 1974 even this last outpost of fixed rates disintegrated, with the announcement by the French that they would float "temporarily" on their own.

Before that happened, there had been one final attempt to get back to fixed exchange rates. A Committee of Twenty was formed to look at ways in which the world monetary system could be patched up. At the 1973 annual meeting of the IMF in Nairobi, the Committee promised a new package by July 1974. Long before that deadline arrived, the oil price rise had made a nonsense of the Committee's deliberations. When it finally reported in the spring of 1974, all it had to show for its work were a few recommendations for rules for floating and for a new reserve unit.

Too much money

The relationship between the collapse of the old monetary system and the acceleration of inflation at the end of the 1960s is still hotly debated among economists and central bankers. Banks have in the past been profoundly wary of floating exchange rates, arguing that they do not "discipline" countries to pursue sensible economic policies. Only if a country has to face the trauma of a devaluation, central bankers sometimes argue, will they take a tough line with trades unions and avoid the temptation to print too much money.

In the concerted boom of 1972–3, central bankers might see the ultimate vindication of this view. But there is a more subtle line of argument that traces the roots of the present inflation back to the fight to defend fixed exchange rates. So keen was the international monetary community to preserve the exchange-rate system of the early 1960s, runs this line, that it went to extravagant lengths to prop it up even when it had become anachronistic. Sterling was buttressed by massive support operations. The dollar was propped up by the willingness of the rest of the world to go on accepting dollars.

The result was that everyone was deluged with money, and particularly with dollars. In three brief years, from 1969 to the end of 1972, the official holdings of reserve assets of all countries rose by an astounding 91 percent. Almost all this rise was in holdings of foreign currencies, which increased as a proportion of total reserves from less than 40 percent in 1969 to just short of 65 percent by the end of 1972. Most of the money was dollars.

Some of the dollars ended up in the hands of central banks, swelling their foreign exchange reserves. With more money in its reserves, it was easier for a country in deficit to put off doing anything about its balance of payments, and for a country in surplus to help out other countries which were in deficit. With more money in the hands of the central banks, in short, it became easier for more countries to run bigger deficits. Surplus countries, on the receiving end of inflows of money, did not always find it easy—and indeed did not always try very hard—to isolate their domestic money supplies from the expansionary effects of an inflow of foreign funds.

There was a second way in which the growing pool of dollars abroad probably contributed to inflation. In the early 1960s it became the foundation of the Eurodollar market. By the late 1960s and the early 1970s, this pool of money was growing with staggering speed and becoming immensely important. It was swollen by the central banks themselves, which often placed their own dollars on deposit with commercial banks.

Enormous and unplanned, the Eurodollar market has made it harder for any national government to control its own money supply. It gives a multinational company a source of funds which is largely outside the control of any single national government. Thus if the American, German and British governments are trying to keep credit tight to slow down the rate at which their economies expand, Ford Motors can still find a way of borrowing money to invest in plants in any of the three countries.

There can be no way back to the world of Bretton Woods. It will be a long time before any central bank tries again to maintain a fixed exchange rate, for the foreign exchange markets have proved themselves stronger than the central banks. In some ways, the collapse of the old monetary order came just in time.

The new regime of floating rates has so far absorbed the extraordinary strains put on it by the huge balance of payments deficits of some industrial countries. The Eurodollar market itself has played a vital role, as a later chapter explains, in directing the surplus revenues of the oil producers to those who need to borrow them.

But the new regime has its weak points, too. The system of floating rates is disconcertingly similar to that of the 1930s, which gave such scope for competitive devaluations. The intricate mechanism of the Eurodollar market links together the banks of the main industrial countries in a way which makes each dependent on the stability of the others. The new monetary order is more volatile than Bretton Woods ever was. As long as the commercial banks continue to trade with each other, and to have confidence in the system, it works; but the very interdependence of the international banking community should make even the boldest banker nervous.

3

Oil Tips the Balance

"Producer power"

The quadrupling of the price of oil was something of a watershed. Without it, the fragile economic situation would have been worrying but not frightening.

If Egypt had not sent her tanks into Sinai on Yom Kippur 1973, and if the Middle East war had never taken place, the OPEC countries might still have raised the price of oil dramatically. Even if they had not done so—even if oil, unlike almost every other commodity, had gone on being cheap—the international economy would still have been in a fragile state in 1974.

There would still have been raging inflation, there would still have been some uncomfortably large balance of payments deficits to be financed, the industrial economies would still have plunged into a dangerous simultaneous recession as governments clamped down on their spending and raised taxation in an effort to slow inflation down. And there might still have been a wages explosion in many countries, as people whose standards of living had fallen or not improved for over a year resisted the transfer of real resources to the commodity producers which the commodity boom entailed.

It is with the oil price rise and the countries which enforced it that this chapter is concerned. Three points stand out. The first is that the rise was long overdue and is not likely fully to be reversed. The age of cheap oil is over for the time being. The second is that when the rise took place, neither the producers nor anyone else had thought through the likely economic and financial implications of dearer oil. The third—and this is a critical point to which this book returns again and again—is that the producers have no hope of spending all their revenues for a very long time to come.

It is only in the last couple of years that power has been in the hands of the producers, for it has only been in the 1970s that the supply and demand conditions for oil have been such that these countries could arbitrarily jack up its price. For the previous twenty years

—throughout the 1950s and the 1960s—the real price fell.

During this period it was the oil companies who took the lead in setting prices. The demand for oil was growing quickly, but the *export* market was still relatively small. America, still the world's largest oil producer today, was then virtually self-sufficient. Indeed, legislation in 1959 effectively shut her market to foreign oil producers. Demand from Japan was rising fast but was still not very big. That meant that in the 1950s and for much of the 1960s Europe was the only big market for exported oil.

So in those years it was the seven giant oil "majors" which called the tune—Shell, British Petroleum, and the five Americans: Exxon (formerly Esso), Gulf, Mobil, Texaco and Socal. In the late 1950s, when the companies unilaterally cut posted oil prices (see Guide to "Oilspeak") by up to 25 percent, the main oil exporters banded together to form OPEC—the Organization of Petroleum Exporting Countries. But it was not until the early 1970s that OPEC began to have a decisive effect on what happened to the price of oil.

In the late 1960s the demand for oil began to catch up with supply. The market in Japan increased. The European countries which had busily run down their coal-mining industries as oil looked cheaper now needed more and more of it. Most important of all, America, which besides being the biggest producer of oil is also the largest consumer, began to import oil in substantial amounts.

With the 1972–3 boom, the demand for oil shot up. In 1970 and 1971 the OPEC governments had already been able to secure big increases in the size of their "take" from the oil companies. Early in 1972 OPEC became more aggressive, and extracted from the companies at a meeting in Geneva an agreement to compensate the producers for losses in revenue resulting from exchange rate changes. In May 1973, after the dollar had been devalued for a second time, they insisted on an improvement in the terms negotiated at Geneva.

OPEC had already begun to feel its power by the summer of 1973. But it took the Arab–Israeli war of October that year to bring home to the producers just how strong their position really was.

It happened almost by coincidence. OPEC had held a meeting in Vienna in mid-September at which it had announced a radical revision of the terms of the agreement that had been reached on oil prices in 1971, an agreement which had been intended to last to the end of 1975. As a result of this meeting the first big oil price rise of 70 percent was announced in Vienna on October 8.

But two days earlier Egypt had invaded Israel. The Arab countries among the twelve members of OPEC make up an inner ring called OAPEC—the Organization of Arab Petroleum Exporting Countries. Ten days after the oil price rise was announced, this group met in

---

A Guide to "Oilspeak"

Equity oil—oil that belongs to the producing company
Buyback oil—oil that belongs to the producing government and is sold back to the producer company
Government retained oil—oil that belongs to the producing government and that it sells to other (i.e., non-producer) companies
Posted price—a reference price on which the amount of tax a company pays to the producer government is based (The company may have to buy back part of the producer government's own oil at this price, too.)
Buyback price—the price at which the company "buys back" buyback oil from the producer government
Auction price—the price at which the producer government sells retained oil to anybody who wants it
Third party price—the price at which the producer company sells oil to other companies

---

Kuwait and decided to cut oil production in order to put pressure on the West to persuade Israel to withdraw from the former Arab territories it occupied. In January the output of the main Arab participants in the cuts—Saudi Arabia, Kuwait, Qatar, Bahrain, Oman, Abu Dhabi and Dubai—was nearly 14 percent below its level in September 1973. Iraq too had cut its production by almost that amount.

These supply cuts (they ended in early spring 1974)

were politically motivated. But their economic effect was devastating. Coming at a time when the demand for oil was still booming, they brought home to everyone the immense power of OPEC. They led to the "market conditions" which the producers then used to justify the further price increase of 130 percent on December 23, 1973.

The producers also used these "market conditions" as an excuse to tear up the agreements on the ownership of the oil which they had negotiated with the companies during the previous two years. Until the late 1960s, most of the oil beneath the Middle East was technically owned by the oil companies who paid royalties or taxes to producer governments for permission to get it out. By 1972–3 most of the producer governments were using their new bargaining power to win new agreements which gave them 51 percent ownership of the oil by the early 1980s. But after the Yom Kippur war these agreements were torn up. During 1974 a new set of agreements were negotiated, most of which increased the producers' share of ownership to 60 percent straight away.

This ultimate demonstration of producer power left the OPEC countries with much more control over both the price of oil and where it was sold than they had had under the oil royalty or tax system. Indeed, by 1975 most Arab countries had moved toward 100 percent ownership.

With the warm winter of 1973–4, the slowdown in

Western economies and the rise in the oil price, demand for oil started to lag behind supply. By the summer of 1974 an oil surplus was building up. The producers began arguing over whether the price of oil should fall back a bit, or whether they should cut production again to keep the price up. Even in the Middle East it was being generally admitted that the price of oil in real terms was not likely to stay as high as it had gone in December 1973. Several countries, notably Iraq, Iran and Saudi Arabia, had ambitious plans to expand their production. The danger with all international cartels is that they tempt individual members to take advantage of the higher prices they achieve by expanding production—thus destroying the effectiveness of the cartel.

OPEC could prove the exception. By spring 1975 the oil price still had not dropped. The consumers need oil more than most OPEC countries need money.

The oil price rise has already led to a reduction in the demand for oil. In the longer run, it will encourage the development of new sources of energy. It may eventually even lead to an energy *glut* and a new era of cheap power. But that day is not likely to come before the Orwellian year of 1984. Until then, the price of oil is likely to keep pace with the prices of other commodities better than it did in the 1950s and 1960s. It may drop back below the peak prices of the second half of 1974, but it will still be high enough to earn vast revenues for the members of OPEC.

Estimated production and revenues

	population (millions)	estimated oil production 1974 (million daily barrels)	estimated oil production 1975 (million daily barrels)
Iran	28.7	6.1	6.0
Saudi Arabia	7.5	8.2	8.0
Iraq	10.1	1.9	2.0
Kuwait	0.9	2.3	1.8
United Arab Emirates	0.2	2.5	2.2
Libya	2.1	1.6	1.4
Algeria	15.3	1.0	1.0
Nigeria	58.0	2.3	2.3
Venezuela	11.0	2.9	2.6
Indonesia	124.9	1.4	1.5

of main OPEC suppliers 1974–5

estimated revenues 1974 (US $ billion)	*estimated revenues 1975 (US $ billion)*	
	low	high
21.2	21.9	23.9
27.9	28.7	31.6
6.5	7.2	7.9
7.8	6.4	7.1
9.1	8.5	9.3
7.4	6.8	7.5
4.9	5.1	5.6
9.9	10.4	11.5
12.6	11.9	13.2
5.2	5.8	6.4

Note: Take per barrel. In 1974 the assumption is made of participation at 60 percent and buyback price at 93 percent of the posted price. The assumption is arbitrary since some countries do not have 60 percent participation and even where it is now the case it has not generally been at this level throughout the year. In 1975 Case 1 assumes OPEC recommendation of uniform price of $9.84 for "marker" crude in the P.G. (Reuter, October 25). Case 2 assumes 100 percent participation and buyback price at 93 percent of the posted price.
N.B.: Take and total revenue in 1975 could be increased by say 15 percent on the amounts shown above to allow for inflation.

Embarrassing riches

These vast revenues will be, for the foreseeable future, much more than the OPEC countries as a group can hope to spend on buying imports of goods and services from the rest of the world. Because the producers cannot spend them, the surplus revenues will pile up to gigantic heights over the years ahead.

The ability of the OPEC countries to spend their new-found wealth varies greatly from country to country. A few will find it easy, but most will find it impossible. The key is population size (see table, which sets out the main exporters together with their populations, estimated production for 1974 and 1975, and estimated revenues for those two years). A glance at some of the bigger producers' economies quickly reveals the core of the difficulty.

Thus the largest oil exporter is Saudi Arabia. It has no earthly hope of employing all its enormous revenues at home in the visible future. Its problem is not just that it has a tiny population; though indeed its population is probably not much bigger than that of Quebec. (The figure of 7.5 million is a World Bank estimate and much higher than figures from other sources—counting nomads is difficult.) But many of Saudi Arabia's scarce citizens would rather wander about the desert than work in a steel mill. And who can blame them?

A lot of money is being pumped into building roads, new ports, and a steel and petro-chemical complex to use the gas that at present simply gets flared off because there is no local use for it. But the contribution of manufacturing to the Saudi Arabian economy is still tiny—just 2 percent of output.

Economists politely refer to the Saudi Arabian difficulty as one of "human infrastructure." It exists in many of the other oil-rich countries, but Saudi Arabia has it in a particularly virulent form. The dilemma is this: If Saudi Arabia wants to build up its industry, it will have to accept tremendous social changes which it does not want. It is still the most conservative of all the major Arab countries. The only way to get a visa there is to be sponsored by a Saudi and present a certificate attesting one's religion. Not that it is a very pleasant place to be. There is no drink (one group of Scottish expatriates in Rhyad brews beer in the bath), no women (women are not even allowed to drive cars)—nothing to spend all that money on. If Saudi Arabia wants to build up its industry, much of that will have to alter. However conservative and cautious Saudi rulers are, however determined to avoid changes, the country's riches will bring them. They will destroy a way of life without putting another in its place. We may in twenty years' time see Saudi Arabia as a sad example of the tragedy of the poor man destroyed by wealth.

Kuwait, too, has a tiny population. After Abu Dhabi it is the world's richest country in terms of GNP per head, and the Kuwaitis never let one forget that. While

Saudi Arabia is the most conservative of the bigger Middle-Eastern producers, Kuwait is the most sophisticated. The bearded Arab dancing in the Beirut nightclub or driving his own Rolls-Royce down London's Kings Road will most likely be a Kuwaiti sheik. This sophistication extends to Kuwait's investment of funds. It is the only one of the oil producers which can talk on absolutely equal terms with Western bankers—as many bankers have found to their dismay.

For Kuwait, as for Saudi Arabia, there is practically no hope of spending the oil money at home. Opportunities to diversify the economy are extremely limited. Because of an acute lack of water, only 3 percent of the land can be cultivated: Most food is imported, and agriculture does not offer much scope for investment. Industry accounts for a tiny fraction—little over 3 percent—of output.

Kuwait is already suffering from two of the problems which afflict many Middle-Eastern producers when they try to spend their revenues at home. One is social. Already, less than half of the population is native Kuwaiti. The rest are immigrants and are firmly treated as second-class citizens: They cannot vote, for example, and have no access to the free health service. The other is inflation. In 1974, soaring prices precipitated a wave of strikes and bankrupted some of the contractors who had undertaken work in Kuwait at fixed prices.

The Middle-Eastern producer with the best hope of

using its oil revenues domestically is Iran. It is second only to Saudi Arabia in oil exports, and the biggest of the Middle-Eastern producers in population. But even Iran finds it has spare funds, and serious difficulty in employing more than part of its cash at home.

Oil accounts for about nine tenths of Iran's export revenue. The country has begun to build up a number of basic industries, such as car manufacture (it makes a version of the Hillman Hunter), basic metals, textiles and petrochemicals. In August 1974 Iran announced that it wanted to increase spending on its fifth five-year development plan by over 90 percent. But there were immediately worries that the country would simply not be able to cope with such an acceleration of the plan. Its infrastructure of ports, roads and railways just did not appear to have the capacity to cope with the 100 percent increase in the volume of imports which the revised plan looked like entailing. There was also likely to be a severe labor problem: An explosive development of industry might drain workers away from agriculture too quickly, creating new social and economic problems.

The three main oil exporters outside the Middle East make an interesting contrast. Venezuela, Nigeria and Indonesia all have large populations and will find it comparatively easy to spend their money as fast as they can earn it. Before the oil price went up, each was running a balance of payments deficit and borrowing hard abroad to pay for development.

Nevertheless, all of them are finding it difficult for their economies to digest sudden wealth. Venezuela is worried by a shortage of skilled workers and technicians, which will slow down industrial growth. As the oil money pours in, Venezuela is also beginning to be plagued by inflation, a disease from which it has been, by South American standards, surprisingly free.

Nigeria is likely to provide an excellent example of how even a country with a large and poor population can have difficulty in spending its oil revenues usefully. It suffers from the endemic problems of developing countries, with a drift of people from the land, rising unemployment (only about 40 percent of the work force actually has a job), and a program of "Nigerianization" which is running up against the inevitable shortage of management skills to replace Europeans and Americans. It has become rich even more recently than most oil producers: Its production is growing in leaps and bounds and is expected to double between the spring of 1974 and the end of 1975. By early 1975 it was already in the same league as Iraq and Libya.

Indonesia, with one of the biggest populations in the world, will have no difficulty at all in spending its oil revenues. Most of its oil is sold to Japan, with some to Australia; but while oil is Indonesia's biggest source of foreign exchange, it also has rubber, timber and immense reserves of minerals. Although Indonesia is still one of the world's poorest countries, it is widely believed in the West that it will be the home of the next economic miracle.

Venezuela, Nigeria and Indonesia are curiosities —the exceptions rather than the rule. The bulk of the world's oil lies underneath the arid and unpopulated countries of the Middle East. It is therefore likely to be many years before all the oil producers spend anything like as much as they earn.

Just how many years is anyone's guess. In 1974 the OPEC countries were probably paid some $95,000 million for their oil. They probably managed to spend about $30,000 million of this on buying goods and services from the rest of the world. That left some $65,000 million spare cash to find a home for. This was in 1974 alone. There is every prospect—even with some fall in the price of oil—that the surpluses will continue to pile up for at least the next ten years.

How big they will grow depends on how fast the capacity of the oil-producing states to absorb imports increases, on how the price of oil moves in relation to other goods, and on how long it takes the rest of the world to develop alternative sources of fuel. One highly conservative attempt to hazard a guess was made by Dr. Jan Tumlir, Director of Research at GATT, in the British *Lloyds Bank Review* for July 1974. He assumed that the oil producers would increase their spending on goods by 25 percent a year from 1974, and on services (in which he included arms) by 35 percent a year. He took it that oil imports would rise by only 2 percent annually, and that the oil producers would be able to earn an annual 10 percent a year on their savings. On that basis, he thought that within five or six years—by the end of the decade—the oil surplus would reach $250,000 million in 1974 prices.

That is an alarming figure—larger than the GNP of France. It is also probably too conservative. For in the decade from 1962 to 1972, the oil producers' total imports increased in *value* by only 7 percent a year. For them to grow in *volume* alone by 25 percent a year from 1974 seems barely conceivable.

This vast oil surplus has devastating consequences. The fact that the producers cannot spend their revenues has helped to push the world into slump. The need for the oil consumers to borrow back the money to cover their huge balance of payments deficits has put a new strain on the weakened international monetary system. The way in which the producers have chosen to invest their cash has put dangerous pressure on the commercial banking system. It is with these consequences of the producers' inability to spend their money that the rest of the book is largely concerned.

4

The Turn of the Screw

A tax on almost everyone

It is widely understood that there is a serious danger of a world slump in 1975–6. It is less well appreciated why this is the case. What has happened, in a nutshell, is this. After several years of accelerating inflation and two of serious overheating, the main industrial countries set out to cure inflation by the traditional, if brutal, expedient of a monetary squeeze. This alone would have guaranteed two lean years—just as the synchronization of expansion in 1972 and 1973 increased the strength of the economic upswing, so the simultaneous deflations all round the world would have reinforced each other. But on top of this monetary squeeze came what was in effect a massive worldwide tax increase, the effect of the oil price rise. It was this price rise that helped push the world towards slump.

Most people think of the oil price rise in terms of its effect on inflation. The rise may have been more violent than those in the prices of other commodities, but it was not much greater. From the end of 1971 to early 1974, zinc, wool and sugar all rose by much the same amount. Like the rise in the prices of other commodities, the rise in the price of oil added, sure enough, to inflation. It did not, however, probably add very much. The OECD calculated in its July 1974 *Economic Outlook* that if the price of oil, including freight and insurance, remained unchanged throughout 1974 at the level of the first quarter, then the two price rises of October and December 1973 would only directly add an average of 1.5 percent to prices in the OECD countries.

But there was one absolutely crucial difference between the rise in the price of oil and the rise in prices of other commodities. It was this. The importing countries could pay the producers of most commodities for their more expensive goods by giving them other goods. So that if the U.S. had to pay Chile more for copper because the price of copper had gone up, then as long as there was spare capacity in the U.S. car industry, the U.S. could always hope to pay Chile for dearer copper by selling the Chileans more U.S. cars. In the short run, the U.S. might perhaps have to run a balance of payments current-account deficit with Chile; in the longer run, provided that the Americans were prepared to accept a temporary check to the rise in their living standards while cars that might have been sold to American customers were exported to Chile, the deficit could be fairly easily removed.

With oil, however, the payment problem was infinitely more complicated. As was explained in chapter 3, many of the richest oil-producing countries are simply incapable of spending their increased revenues at anything like the speed they pile up.

So the way the oil price rise hit the industrial world was like this. People found themselves having to spend a bigger chunk of their incomes on oil—on running their cars, heating their houses, and so on. Companies also found themselves hit, paying more for fuel and for raw materials with an oil base. Both people and companies, in other words, were worse off—as if they had been subjected to a tax that was as large as the oil price rise.

This money—the equivalent of the tax revenue—ended up in the hands of the oil producers. For the U.S. it showed in the form of the oil deficit in the balance of payments; for the oil producers, it showed in their massive current-account surpluses, and their huge surplus revenues. If they had been Indians or

Malaysians, with expensive development programs and vast poverty-stricken populations, or if they had been developed countries like Australia or Canada, they would no doubt have spent these revenues quickly on buying goods from countries like the U.S. For less than a year American workers would have found that their standard of living did not improve, while goods were sold abroad to pay off the higher oil price. After that, making goods to sell to the oil producers would have meant more jobs for American workers, and more profits for American companies. A transfer of real resources equivalent to rather less than one year's normal growth would have paid off the rise in the oil bill.

Because the oil producers could not spend all their revenues, the oil price rise dug a deflationary hole in the industrial economies. People and companies spent more of their money on more expensive oil. There was less money around to buy goods and services produced in America. And the increase in demand from the oil-producing countries was nowhere near enough to provide an attractive market for these goods and services.

It was as if the U.S. government had imposed a big increase in indirect taxation, such as a sales tax, on the whole country—and then handed the entire takings over to the oil states. Worse, it was as if every industrial and developing country *except* the oil states had imposed huge taxes on their countries—and handed the money to OPEC. Not only did people in America have less money to spend on U.S.-produced goods and services, so that companies had to struggle harder to find markets and have had eventually to lay people off. People all over the world have found themselves with less money—less money to buy their own industries' goods, less money to buy each other's exports. Because it affected every country, the effect of the oil "tax" has been twice as severe as it would have been if it had only affected one. At the very moment when each country has needed to export more, export markets all over the world have suddenly contracted.

If countries had accepted the deflationary effect of the oil price rise and left it at that, 1974 and 1975 would have been uncomfortable enough. Coming after many months in which, thanks to the need to pay higher commodity prices, living standards had not risen, the higher oil price would have put strains on most countries' economies.

But the oil consumers promptly set out to make things very much worse. They could have accepted the deflationary effect of the oil price rise, and forgone the equivalent of a year or so's normal growth. They could even have offset it, by deliberately putting back into their economies some or all of the demand that the producers had taken out. They could, for example, have cut taxes on fuel by as much as the producers had raised its price—in which case people and companies would have had just as much spending power as before the price rise. But governments took neither course. With the possible exception of the U.K., they *added* to the deflationary effect of the price increase—they took out of their economies *still more* than the oil producers had done. They cut public spending, they raised taxes, and they curbed credit. The share of responsibility of governments for the slump of 1975–6 is not everywhere the same. In some countries, such as Britain and Japan, where the extra cost of imported oil is high relative to the size of the whole economy, the deflationary effects of the oil price increase have been considerable. In other countries—and the United States is the most notable example—the extra cost of imported oil is relatively small. The fall in GNP in the United States in 1974 was very largely the result of earlier changes in taxation and monetary policy taken to fight inflation.

An unbalanced world

Why did the industrial world risk recession, when the dangers were perfectly well understood and widely discussed? The answer is that in 1974 some of the industrial countries had strong balances of payments and some had weak. Those in a strong position could have expanded their economies, but regarded inflation as a more terrifying danger than recession. Those in a weak position might have liked to expand, but dared not take risks when they were having to borrow immense sums of money to cover their deficits. So the chance to avoid a slump was missed.

Even before the rise in the oil price, a serious imbalance had begun to emerge among the industrial countries. Some were sliding deep into balance of payments deficit, and others into surplus. Thus in 1973 Britain, Japan and Italy were in heavy deficit; Germany, the Netherlands and the United States had begun to move into considerable surplus. There seem to have been several reasons for this divergence, but perhaps the main one was that the deficit countries took longer to slow their economies down after the 1972–3 boom than did the surplus countries. Even after the rise in the oil price began to affect balances of payments, in the early months of 1974 the non-oil trade balances of Germany and the U.S.A. initially continued to improve, while those of Italy, Britain and Japan still deteriorated.

In 1974 this problem became much more severe. A new imbalance—that between the oil producers and the rest of the world—was imposed on the existing problem. At the end of 1974 the unspent surplus of the oil producers for the year appeared to add up to about $55,000 million. Arithmetic dictates that every surplus has to be matched by a deficit somewhere else. The developing countries were expected to have current-account deficits adding up to rather less than $20,000 million. The remainder was expected to be run by the industrial countries.

When early in 1974 the Secretariat of the OECD

tried to work out how this remaining current-account deficit would be shared out among the industrial countries of the West, it came on a disturbing fact. Adding up the forecasts that individual OECD countries had made of the current-account deficits they expected to run in 1974, it found that they came to half the total the OECD was forecasting. In other words, the individual industrial countries in early 1974 were underestimating the average size of their current-account deficits by 100 percent.

This extraordinary over-optimism is easy enough to explain. Country after country realized that, thanks partly to the oil price rise and partly to restrictive government policies, its economy would be operating below full capacity in 1974. Country after country, seeing the devastating effect of the rise in the oil price on its balance of payments, solemnly explained to its citizens that there would be a need "to leave room for export growth" or that "the rise in exports would be the main source of growth" in 1974. Few stopped to realize that policies which might be logical enough for one country in isolation were utterly self-defeating if pursued all over the world.

But quite apart from self-delusion, there was another danger in the industrial countries' balance of payments positions. It was this. Nearly three quarters of the entire $40,000 million deficit, it was clear by mid-1974, would fall on the shoulders of four industrial countries: Britain, Italy, Japan and France. On the basis of the OECD's mid-year reckoning, France would run a current-account deficit of $6,200 million; Japan of $7,750 million; Italy of $8,750 million; and Britain of $9,750 million.

There were several smaller countries which also expected deficits which, if not vast in absolute terms, were huge in relation to the size of their economies. Greece, Ireland, Norway, Denmark and Finland all could expect to run deficits of more than 3 percent of their Gross National Products.

At the other extreme, there were a few industrial countries expecting to run surpluses. America could expect to remain close to overall balance. It had swung, between 1972 and 1973, from a deficit of $8,400 million to a surplus of $3,000 million, and by the beginning of 1974, the American current surplus was as large as Germany's. Then it began to fall back but its small deficit in 1974 as a whole came nowhere near reflecting the $13,000 million increase in its oil bill. True, the U.S. will run a larger deficit in 1975. But, oil apart, the U.S. balance of payments current account remained strong in 1974.

So did the current accounts of two other countries. Germany in the first half of 1974 was already running a current-account surplus at an annual rate of over $10,000 million—two-and-a-half times the size of the record surplus of 1973. The Benelux group also expected to be strongly in surplus in 1974—led by the Netherlands which, with an economy less than a fifth the size of Germany's, expected a surplus about a sixth the size of the German one.

He who pays the piper

It was widely agreed immediately after the oil price rise that there was no point in countries trying to deflate to get rid of their oil deficits. To do so would merely shuffle the deficits between each other. In January 1974 the Committee of Twenty, which had been set up to work out a plan to reform the world's money system, met in Rome. It was a high-powered meeting of Finance Ministers and central bankers, and it quickly turned into a seminar on The World After the Oil Price Rise.

The ministers recognized that for some time the world was going to have to live with the oil producers' unspendable surpluses, and that if the industrial countries reacted to their new and increased balance of payments deficits by any of the traditional ploys of deflating, devaluing or slapping on import controls they would simply pass on the deficit to other oil-importing countries. The sensible thing, it seemed, would be to think of the balance of payments of each country in two parts—an ordinary "non-oil" deficit or surplus, to be dealt with in the traditional way; and a new "oil" deficit, which would be the counterpart of the oil producers' own unspendable surplus revenues. The correct way to handle the oil part of each country's balance of payments would be to accept it, and to finance it by borrowing back from the oil producers the revenues which they themselves could not yet spend. In time, the producers' economies would develop to a point where the surplus revenues *could* be spent—and then the transfer of real resources from the industrial world to pay the extra price of oil would take place.

So this part of the problem would be handled by "recycling" the oil revenues. How this is working in practice is described in the next chapter. It appeared at first that the ministers had gone a stage further. They seemed to have recognized that even if the right policy for the world as a whole was to accept the oil deficit, some countries were already running big balance of payments deficits and would want to take steps to get rid of their non-oil deficits. They would only be able to do so if the countries which were in non-oil surplus helped to make it possible, by deliberately expanding their own economies by *at least* as much as the deflationary effect of the oil price rise would contract them. In other words, Germany and America would have to reflate and run balance of payments deficits equivalent to the additional cost of their oil imports. Only that way would there be expanding export markets in which countries like Britain and Italy could sell enough exports to reduce their non-oil deficits.

It was here that things began to go wrong. For the largest single economy in the industrial world, the United States of America, did not see things quite this way; and neither did the country with the biggest balance of payments surplus, Germany. Both Mr. George Shultz, then U.S. Treasury Secretary, and Mr. Helmut Schmidt, then German Finance Minister, had two reasons for disagreeing with this policy prescription.

First, they argued that it would be wrong to try to accommodate the oil price increase. The surplus oil revenues would build up, in the hands of the producer countries, an intolerable mountain of claims on the resources of the oil-consuming countries. When the oil producers spent their revenues, they would create impossible pressures on the industrial capacity of the oil-consuming countries. So the two countries preferred not to work out a way of coping with dearer oil—in the hope that by doing so they would put pressure on the oil producers to roll back their prices.

Secondly, Germany and America took a different view of the solution to inflation from some of the other industrial countries. They argued (as indeed did Japan) that their experience had been that inflation was basically the result of too much demand chasing too few goods. The cure, as they saw it, was to reduce demand—to deflate, and let their economies grow more slowly.

Some of the other industrial countries violently disagreed. The British, in particular, argued anxiously in the spring and summer of 1974 that their experience had been that deflation might actually make things *worse*. Already, thanks to the commodity price boom, real incomes had not grown since summer 1973. Now, frightened by the prospect of financial uncertainty, people might demand higher wages more aggressively—there might be a "wages explosion," eventually driving unemployment up higher than it would otherwise have gone. Companies operating below full capacity would find their unit costs increased and would have to put up prices by more than they would otherwise have done. "Demand pull" inflation would be replaced by the "cost push" variety. As far as the British government could see, there was no level of unemployment "politically acceptable" at which inflation was actually likely to be dampened.

There was evidence, by summer 1974, of the same problem in the U.S.A. After a year of falling real wages, American trades unions began demanding bigger pay increases. But the Administration ignored this. So, as 1974 passed, the U.S.A. and Germany did not expand their economies by enough to offset the contractionary effects of the oil price rise. For a long time neither took any action at all to reflate.

The big industrial countries faced a no-win game. To expand demand with price rises already running in double figures would have been to risk runaway completely uncontrollable inflation. To deflate might also have meant, for some, a risk of worsening inflation, and made world slump a virtual certainty for all. By the autumn of 1974, the governments of the major industrial countries had already taken the decisions which were likely to set the course of their economies through 1975 and into 1976. Attempts to change course would only affect what happened after that.

The "no-win" game

The industrial world marched firmly over the brink, led by the U.S.A. The vast size of the American economy—about half the size of the total economy of the OECD area—made it inevitable that it should determine what happened to the rest of the world. Equally important, the problems which the deficit countries faced in borrowing enough money to balance the books left them in no position to take an independent line.

When President Gerald Ford took over from President Nixon in August 1974 he quickly made it clear which side he was on. That he backed cuts in public spending was hardly surprising. Dr. Arthur Burns, chairman of the Federal Reserve Board, had been calling for a reduction of $10,000 million in budget spending. He was joined by Dr. Herbert Stein, the outgoing chairman of the Council for Economic Advisers, by Dr. Stein's successor, Mr. Alan Greenspan, and by Mr. William Simon, Nixon's Secretary of the Treasury, in arguing that America needed a prolonged period of stagnation, with unemployment around 5½ percent for several years on end, to cure inflation permanently. Mr. Simon even said privately that he would be prepared to see unemployment reach 9 percent.

Even before the conservative Mr. Ford became President, the U.S. Federal Reserve had been adopting a progressively stricter monetary policy, and fiscal policy had been designed to work the same way. When the budget for fiscal year 1975 had been drawn up under Nixon, it had been expected to run the same surplus, on a full employment basis, as in fiscal 1974. In other words, the budget had never been designed to offset any of the deflationary effect of the oil price rise at all.

Not surprisingly, real growth in the first half of 1974 was some 3½ percent down (at an annual rate) on the last half of 1973. It fell again in the second half. Real incomes fell in the first six months of the year and did not recover much in the next six months. Unemployment was growing, and looked like reaching nearly 9 percent in 1975.

While the U.S.A. continued to deflate, Germany showed little haste in trying to expand a sluggish economy. True, after beginning 1974 with a tight money policy, the Bundesbank gradually slackened up a little as the months went by and the German balance of payments surplus stubbornly outgrew all predictions. By the summer, interest rates had started to edge down from record heights. Fiscal policy also began to be relaxed. In summer 1974, an income tax reform program was passed to come into effect at the beginning of 1975, cutting tax revenues by the equivalent of nearly 1 percent of GNP.

It was on exports that Germany depended in 1974 to keep the economy moving. But that was hardly enough. By the middle of the year, unemployment had already risen to its highest level since 1956 and by the end, almost one million people were out of work.

With huge deficits to finance and volatile foreign exchange markets to worry about, the countries which were most heavily in deficit now had no choice. Some of them indeed, in spite of murmurs of disapproval from the others, embarked on determinedly "beggar-my-neighbor" policies. Japan was the worst offender: But Japan had the worse inflation problem, and the best reason to believe that by restraining demand and letting unemployment rise, it could tame inflation.

So Japanese demand management became progressively tighter until by the spring of 1974 industrial output was falling dramatically. Real GNP probably dropped at an annual rate of nearly 9½ percent in the first half of 1974. Monetary policy, as in America and Germany, again carried the brunt of slowing the economy down. Ceilings on bank credit were repeatedly tightened during the summer of 1974, and reserve requirements on bank lending repeatedly increased. The Japanese, like so many other countries, pinned their main hope of growth on exports: Unlike many others, they had embarked by the autumn of 1974 on an export drive of ferocious determination.

The French went one better. When everyone was

inveighing sternly against the dangers of competitive devaluation, 1930s style, the French announced in January 1974 that they were abandoning years of faith in fixed exchange rates and letting the franc float. Inevitably, it sank.

At the same time the French government took a staunchly restrictive stand. In June, the government announced a continuation of the existing credit squeeze, and this was followed by a rise in the banks' lending rates. It also cut public spending and increased company and personal income taxes. As the French economy was still quite buoyant in the first half of 1974, it looked as though these would have their main effect in the first months of 1975.

Only two countries argued that international deflation was being overdone, and would lead to slump in 1975: Italy and Britain. But as Italy's economy was in such a shambles that nobody wanted to lend it any money, and as Britain looked like running the world's largest current-account deficit, neither was in a position to do much about redressing the balance.

Italy ran into trouble late in February when the government applied to the IMF for a loan. The loan was only offered on condition that Italy clamp down on its expansive fiscal and monetary policy. There was a government crisis, and subsequently, as the balance of payments continued to get rapidly worse and inflation to accelerate, the Italians introduced direct controls on imports. By this time—in May—Italy was already finding it virtually impossible to raise money on the Eurocurrency market, and Italy had to pledge its gold as security for a German loan.

The British, thanks to the inflow of Middle-Eastern money into the City, found it easier to cover their balance of payments deficit. Indeed it put them in the unique position, in the early summer of 1974, of having by far the largest deficit ever—and a strengthening exchange rate. But it was only in July that Mr. Healey took any steps of deliberate expansion, and then they were of necessity extremely cautious. They seemed unlikely to prevent unemployment from rising in the autumn of 1974 and from getting close to a million in 1975.

Many other industrial countries bowed to the inevitable. In Canada, monetary policy was tightened and interest rates pushed to record levels in July 1974. In New Zealand, where a massive turnaround from balance of payments surplus to deficit threatened to exhaust foreign exchange reserves within a month, the government ordered major cuts in public spending in August and devalued in September. In South Africa, a credit squeeze had been introduced early in 1974. In Belgium, fiscal policy was tightened. There were few exceptions. In Australia, after introducing a budget which raised excise duties and postal charges and cut some welfare programs in July, the government then determinedly resisted attempts by the Treasury to persuade it to take further deflationary action. In Norway and the Netherlands, fiscal policy was deliberately relaxed to counteract the contractionary effect of dearer oil.

The sum total of these government decisions, together with the effect on world demand of the oil price rise, would in any case make 1975 and 1976 two unpleasant years. They would be years when living standards continued to stagnate, as they did in 1973 and 1974, or even declined. They would be years of considerable social tensions in many countries, as each section of society tried to make sure that it did not have to take a cut in living standards, by trying to increase its income at the expense of other groups—where white collar workers found a new militancy, where trades unions became more aggressive, where government policies to redistribute income from the better off to the worse off came under severe attack.

But 1975 and 1976 could yet be worse than that. For the policies of the deficit countries will be determined very largely by their ability to borrow enough money to cover their huge oil bills. Once their credit runs out —once nobody wants either to lend to them or to hold their currencies—they will have little choice but to slap on import controls, curb capital movements and return to the restrictions which crucified the world economy in the 1930s. It is this problem of recycling the oil revenues to the countries which need them that the next chapter takes up.

5

Coping With the Oil Billions

Why recycling matters

The unspent oil billions do not just threaten the world with recession. They also represent the biggest investment problem in world history. The core of the problem, as we have seen, is to find a way of paying the producers for their oil. They cannot absorb enough goods now to square the bill, but they will want the goods in the future. In the meantime they need investments which will keep their value and be eroded neither by inflation nor by fluctuations in exchange rates. If they cannot find them, they will be more sensible to keep their oil in the ground.

But there is a clash of interest between the oil producers and the oil consumers. If the producers invest their money where it is safest, they will invest it in the countries which have least need to import oil, the strongest balances of payments, and the soundest currencies. But those are exactly the countries which least need to borrow money from the producers. The countries which need to borrow most urgently are the countries with huge deficits, like Britain, Italy and France—and the wretched developing countries, whose reserves are slimmest.

Ideally, the handling of this delicate situation needs the maximum international cooperation. It calls for all the machinery of international financial consultation which has been developed since the Second World War. It has received neither. The main recycling effort has been left to commercial banks operating in the Euromarkets. But the Euromarkets were never designed for the job. The strains this has placed on these banks are dealt with in the next chapter. We now look at the way in which recycling has been operating, and at the dilatory attempts of the international monetary community to provide an alternative to the Euromarkets.

All that money to invest

The Arab oil producers are in the same position as a poor man who has just won a lottery: He starts by saying that nothing will change, he then goes out and buys everything he wants, and later he looks around for investments that will give him a steady income into his old age. That is where his troubles start. Ideally he would like to put the money into his own business but he is worried he hasn't got the necessary business skills to make a go of it. If on the other hand he invests his money, how is he to know he won't get swindled? There are plenty of sharp investment advisers around with little schemes they want him to put his money in. He ends by being so bewildered that he simply keeps his money on deposit with a bank . . . and sees inflation steadily whittle it away.

This is precisely what the oil producers have gone through; they want to invest the money in their own countries, but these countries cannot absorb investment funds fast enough. They do not trust the advice offered them on what to do with their investment funds because they have been taken for a ride in the past; so they simply put their money on deposit with one of the top twenty or so world banks.

The producers have three main worries in deciding where to deposit their cash. The worst has been that inflation would whittle away the value of their savings. Ideally, the oil producers would no doubt have liked to put their money into some kind of index-linked security, whose capital value or interest rate was regularly adjusted to allow for inflation. But the industrial countries have been wary of borrowing on that basis—partly because even the record levels of interest rates charged on conventional borrowing have looked cheap when compared with the rate of inflation, and partly because they have been worried about spreading indexation to their own domestic economies.

The second dilemma facing the oil producers has been what to do about floating exchange rates. They quickly realized that the amounts of money under their control were so vast that if they decided to sell out of a currency in which there was a thin market, they could easily cause the exchange rate to fall drastically—and so find themselves locked in.

The third problem is one with which the oil producers have long been familiar—from the other side of the fence. It is nationalization. The oil producers know well the hostilities which can be aroused when a foreign investor buys substantial interests in the industry and real estate of a country. They do not want to expose themselves to the same treatment as they have meted out to the oil companies.

The first instinct of some Middle-Eastern producers, faced with the prospect of a torrent of oil money, was to try, by setting up barter deals with their customers, to reduce the amount of cash they would receive. Thus Britain, France and Japan were quick to sign up with some of the producers—Iran in particular—to exchange industrial and capital goods for oil. The details varied, but the deals usually had two elements: The oil country supplied oil for several years, and the industrial country supplied industrial goods (usually capital goods such as factories or power stations) in return. The oil producer might also place spare funds with the industrial country in the form either of deposits or of a loan.

To the producer, the attraction of barter deals is that they offer real goods in exchange for oil—not just depreciating paper money. For the consumer, a barter deal offers security of supply, and makes it harder for the producer suddenly to raise the price. But barter deals do nothing to reduce the piling up of surplus oil funds. If Iran buys a nuclear power station or two from France in a barter deal she may have less money to invest, but equally she has fewer things to spend money on. Every power station bought by barter is one less power station to be bought with money.

If the oil producers found it hard to spend the oil revenues as fast as they earned them, other developing countries did not; and an early way of disposing of some of the money was to lend it to less lucky Third World countries. Sometimes the producers offered oil at concessionary rates. More often they paid money into special funds set up for the purpose.

Among the first countries to benefit were Egypt and Syria, two Arab states with no oil of their own. As these two countries were the main protagonists in the Israeli wars, cynics in the Arab world see the oil-rich countries as paying someone else to do their fighting for them. Some take this argument a stage further. "Do you want to know when the next Middle East war is coming?"

they ask. "Look for Syria's foreign exchange reserves. As soon as they start to run low, Syria will attack Israel and get the oil producers to foot the bill."

But these two outlets use only a fraction of the spare funds that the oil producers are accumulating. What has been happening to the bulk that remains? With $1,500,000,000 coming in every week, the producers have simply popped most of it in the bank. Even the most sophisticated producer, Kuwait, has taken this course. Kuwait was one of the first producers to become super-rich. By the time of the 1973 oil price increases, it had already spent everything it could in Kuwait itself. It had a free medical service, free schools, free universities, plenty of roads, a new airport and so on. There was even a scheme that gave every Kuwaiti a plot of land to do what he liked with. Anything to get rid of the money that kept flooding in.

Then in the first part of 1974 there was no possible way in which they could go on using the funds at home. The money was piling up at the rate of about $140 million a week. The Kuwaitis bought an office block in the Champs-Elysées in Paris, and put millions into a fund for Arab economic development. Still the funds grew. They put deposits, usually at very short term, with a handful of top London banks. Finally in desperation Kuwait placed close to $2,350 million in U.K. government securities during the first half of 1974, so saving sterling from a further slump and rescuing the Bank of England from the uncomfortable task of trying to finance the U.K. government deficit at a time when no one else would touch gilts.

By mid-1974 the Kuwait Investment Office in London, which handles much of the funds, felt that its *ad hoc* method of deciding what to do with its money had gone far enough. It asked—who else?—the Bank of England for advice on how to run its investments. Gradually, the money it deposited with banks was put out for longer terms. The Kuwaitis also began to look around for property—preferably office blocks in prime locations—in an organized way. Finally they started looking for suitable companies in Europe and America to buy. The first was the U.K. St. Martin's Property Corporation.

Saudi Arabia, by contrast, has shown few signs of investing its funds long-term. Their equivalent of the KIO (but in Saudi Arabia) is the Saudi Arabian Monetary Authority. During 1974 SAMA placed most of its funds—dollars because Saudi oil is paid for in dollars—either on deposit with about twenty international banks or in U.S. Treasury bills, through the Federal Reserve Bank of New York.

The Fed found that enormous amounts of money were collecting, and that there were no instructions on what to do with it. After a while the Saudis agreed to start placing it on deposit with large New York and other banks. Two banks, Chase Manhattan and Morgan Guaranty, got the lion's share of these funds.

The investment policies of other Arab producers

have followed much the same pattern, the bulk of the money going into bank accounts but a few cautious millions gradually trickling through into shares or property. Almost all the money found its way, in the first instance at least, into the huge money markets of London and New York, and was deposited either in sterling, or in domestic dollar accounts, or in Eurodollars. Where the money has gone has depended to a surprising extent on habit, and on who has been advising the country on its investment. Several of the producers—Kuwait, and the other Persian Gulf countries and Nigeria—belong to the Sterling Area. They have tended to hold the bulk of their money in sterling.

Putting money on deposit with the biggest banks in the largest money markets is, from the producers' point of view, a low-risk policy. A large bank is more likely to be stable; and the money, provided it is not tied up for too long, can always be switched into another currency if interest rates or exchange rates begin to move the wrong way. But this policy is not, in the long term, in the best interests of either the producers or the consumers.

It has been left to a non-Arab producer, Iran, to demonstrate a more profitable alternative. Iran was the pacesetter in two kinds of investment in the first part of 1974—direct loans to Western governments, and direct stakes in Western industry. By lending $1,200 million to the British government in the form of a medium-term loan, the Shah was really doing the same thing as Kuwait did when it bought $1,170 million of medium-term U.K. government securities. But the Iranian loan was specifically made for several years, whereas the Kuwait investment could in theory be withdrawn immediately. In fact it would be very difficult for the Kuwaitis to sell their securities without the help of the Bank of England, as the sudden withdrawal of that amount would push the sterling exchange rate downwards and so reduce the value of their securities. For the lender, the advantage of making a medium-term loan is that it in theory gets a higher rate of interest and the capital value of its loan, in money terms at least, is safe.

Iran's other main innovation was to take substantial equity interests in Western industry. The first example of such a deal was the 25 percent shareholding it took in the German steel firm of Krupp in July 1974. By taking shareholdings in Western companies, the oil producers could buy a real stake in the technology and industry of the developed world. They also bought a say in the way their investments were managed. Thus the Krupp deal gave Iran a seat on the supervisory board, while the fact that Iran had bought so large a stake made sure that it would have real influence on the way Krupp was run.

Both the government to government loans and direct investments in industry and property may well become increasingly common as the oil producers accustom themselves to their new wealth. But it is likely to be a long time before the bulk of the revenues do not end up being lent out to commercial banks, which in turn relend them through the Euromarkets. When the oil price first rose, there was no shortage of grandiose schemes for this recycling to be carried on through official agencies. But the signs are that none of these plans will get very far.

Queuing up to borrow

Probably the ideal way to handle recycling would be through international agencies, which would borrow money directly from the oil producers and lend them on to the countries which needed the money. When the price of oil was first increased, academics all over the world threw themselves enthusiastically into the task of designing machinery to do this. It was clearly realized that a high priority for the oil producers in choosing how to invest their cash would be anonymity and security. It was realized, too, that the oil surpluses would provide a huge pool of funds which nervous investors might switch from one currency to another, producing foreign exchange crises which would make the runs on the dollar and the pound in the late 1960s look trivial by comparison.

So there were plans for giant unit trusts, and plans to sell the oil producers the central banks' stock of gold. There were plans to recycle through the IMF, plans to recycle through the Bank for International Settlements, and an ingenious if complicated British scheme devised by Mr. Harold Lever, Chancellor of the Duchy of Lancaster, under which the oil-consuming countries would only pay over the money for their oil when the producers were able to spend it.

None came to much. By late 1974 only one scheme was anything more than pie in the sky. It had first been outlined in Rome in January 1974, by Dr. Johannes Witteveen, managing director of the IMF, at a meeting of the Committee of Twenty, the body which had originally been set up to devise a reform of the world's monetary system. Dr. Witteveen suggested that the Fund would borrow money from the producers and re-lend it, at something like commercial rates of interest.

The scheme was slow to get off the ground. Part of the problem was that the U.S.A. never gave it wholehearted blessing. The Americans, anxious to get tough with the producers and sure in any case of a substantial flow of oil money into the relatively strong dollar, were unenthusiastic about a plan which would be a deliberate attempt to accommodate, rather than to challenge, the higher oil price. Another part of the Witteveen scheme's difficulties was to choose an interest rate which gave the oil producers an adequate rate of return but did not look alarmingly high to borrowers. Finally, the scale of the scheme was grossly inadequate. Its planned size for the whole of 1974 was a mere $3,600 million, just three weeks' surplus revenues.

Two other schemes were agreed upon in the first weeks of 1975. The first was a sort of revised version of the IMF scheme already in operation. It had been proposed at the 1974 Fund meeting by Mr. Denis Healey, the U.K. Chancellor of the Exchequer, and a committee had been set up under Mr. John Turner, the Canadian finance minister, to study it. Under this scheme, the oil producers would deposit funds with the IMF, which would lend them on, at commercial rates of interest and for periods of five to seven years, to industrial countries in balance of payments difficulties. The Common Market countries hoped that this scheme would be in operation by Easter 1975, handling perhaps $7,000 million of oil money.

The second scheme also agreed upon was put forward in autumn 1974 by Dr. Henry Kissinger, the U.S. Secretary of State. Under it, the industrial countries with which the oil producers deposited surplus funds would club together to bail out other developed countries in balance of payments difficulties. The Common Market countries argue that the Kissinger scheme would need legislation in many countries to operate, so that it could not be in operation before the end of 1975. But they agreed to go ahead with the Kissinger scheme, in exchange for American cooperation on the IMF scheme.

While schemes for recycling through international institutions were being discussed and getting slowly off the ground, the deficit countries became increasingly desperate for funds. They began by borrowing vast amounts on the Eurocurrency markets.

Some of them had been doing so before the oil price made their plight desperate. The concept of borrowing on the Euromarkets to cover a balance of payments deficit was pioneered by Dr. Guido Carli, the Governor of the Bank of Italy, two or three years before the oil price rise. A steady stream of Italian public utilities made their way to the Eurocurrency market and borrowed larger and larger sums. Dr. Carli's example was followed in 1972 by the British, who borrowed initially through their local authorities and then through nationalized industries.

The developing countries had also flocked to the market to borrow money in 1972 and 1973. For them, it was not cheap money—it certainly cost more than money from the World Bank's concessionary loan fund, the International Development Agency (IDA). But it was readily obtainable money, at a time when aid programs were hardly expanding, and it was money with no strings attached. A five-year loan on the Eurodollar market did not bring with it a posse of bureaucrats from Washington, intent on making sure that the money was used for the purposes it had been lent for, or that the country's economy was being properly run.

Early in 1974 the game intensified. The developing countries, hard hit by the higher oil price, began to drop out of the line of borrowers. But governments in the developed world faced with massive deficits now began to borrow from the market directly as well as through their front organizations, the public authorities. The two largest borrowings in the history of the market were made directly by governments. In spring 1974 the French borrowed $1,500 million and a few weeks later the British topped that by arranging a loan of $2,500 million. These loans helped to swell total borrowings to extraordinary amounts.

In the first six months of 1974 alone, Britain borrowed a staggering $4,795 million on the Eurocurrency market. France borrowed $2,924 million and Italy $2,240 million. Together, these three countries accounted for no less than half of all known Eurocurrency credits. The bulk of the money—some 87 percent—was borrowed by official institutions or guaranteed by them. In other words, almost all the loans were government-backed. Meanwhile, the developing countries were pushed aside. In 1973 they had accounted for 41 percent of all Eurocurrency borrowings. In the first half of 1974 their share fell to only 30 percent.

As a result of these huge loans, total borrowings in the Euromarket in the first half of 1974 were not far short of the $22,000 million borrowings for the whole of 1973—itself more than twice the figure for 1972, which was in turn double the level of borrowings for 1971. How, bankers soon began to wonder, could this money ever be repaid? All these huge loans are, after all, on the balance sheets of commercial banks. If they are not repaid, the banks themselves will be wiped out.

6

The Cowardice of Money

Where did it all go?

In May 1931 an Austrian bank collapsed. It was called the Kredit Anstalt, a name then unknown outside Austria. The collapse was to set off a string of bank failures around the world, but particularly in neighboring Germany and in America. By the middle of 1931 the world was already well into the Great Depression. The failure of banks was the effect, not the cause, of falling production and profits. But it was the failure of banks—together with the decline in stock market values—that stopped the world from recovering from the depression. For, after confidence in the world's capital markets had been destroyed, it became impossible for industry to raise funds and get the world economy moving once more.

Will it happen again? Even before it had to carry the strain of recycling the oil funds, the financial system of the 1970s had been weakened. Two years of money galore had been succeeded, with breathtaking speed, by an international credit squeeze of extraordinary severity. The boom years of 1972–3 came at the end of a period when the world's money supply had soared. International liquidity between the end of 1969 and the end of 1973 had grown by over 140 percent. This international mone, boom had its parallel in some individual countries. Then, in the autumn of 1973, the taps were suddenly turned off. One government after another, desperately worried by inflation, tightened monetary policy. In some countries where the government was weak—as in Italy or America—the central bank stepped into a political vacuum to fight inflation with its own weapons of credit control.

Even when money was easily available, interest rates had looked high by historical standards. With rapid inflation, this was understandable: When prices are rising at 10 percent a year, any interest rate of *less* than 10 percent gives the lender no compensation even for the ravages of inflation. But once the world's central banks, led by the U.S. Federal Reserve, decided to conduct their own attack on inflation, interest rates soared.

The effect was to put the financial system under considerable pressure. As money became harder to find, fewer people could afford assets such as property or shares—and as interest rates rose, more people wanted to put their cash into fixed interest securities or bank deposits to take advantage of the higher yields.

The slide in equity values was the most dramatic reflection of dearer money. Share prices had begun their slide in stock markets all over the world in the closing months of 1972. In 1973 the downward drift had continued. By early 1975 it brought share prices on the London market, one of the worst hit, down to levels last touched in the late 1950s—levels, indeed, which after allowing for inflation had not been seen since the mid-1920s—*before* the first Great Crash.

Other exchanges fared little better. The Dow Jones index in New York lost more than one third of its value between the beginning of 1973 and autumn 1974; the Sydney exchange hit a 12-year low in August 1974; the Tokyo index did much the same; Paris, Johannesburg, Frankfurt and Sydney all fell by between 30 and 50 percent, while the Hang Seng index in Hong Kong fell from 1,800 at the height of an insane boom in early 1973 to close to 300. In fact the last country where the decline in equity values took place was the country whose economy was regarded with most suspicion, not to say despair, abroad—namely Italy. In August 1974 the *Il Sole* index on the Milan stock exchange was still standing at double the level of early 1973. Yet more surprisingly its peak was in March 1974, at the very height of the energy crisis!

Quite suddenly in autumn 1974 Italian share prices collapsed too. Gloom was unbroken. Almost everywhere almost everybody with shares lost a lot of money.

Explaining the collapse of share prices is not easy (and if we could do so, we would hardly give the answer away for these few modest pennies). But three factors probably go to make up the answer. The most important was probably the rise in interest rates, and the monetary squeeze, which made the return on money invested in shares look low compared with money invested in cash. A second was the belief that equity holdings might prove a worse way of hedging against inflation than investment in real assets—such as property, land, and houses, and works of art and antiques. Perhaps a third was the deepening gloom with which, in 1974, the share markets regarded the world's economic future.

The effect of the collapse of share prices was to make it virtually impossible for companies to raise new equity capital from the stock exchanges. But they could hardly expect to carry on their investment plans simply from retained profits, particularly since the outlook for profits became worse and worse. Increasingly firms turned to the banks. Through the late 1960s there already seems to have been a rise in company gearing—in the proportion of money that firms borrowed on a fixed-interest basis, instead of raising on the equity market. OECD figures (analyzed in *Euromoney*, August 1974) suggested that between 1967 and 1971 the gearing of non-financial companies had been increasing in America, Britain, Germany and Italy. In Japan it had been falling—but then it was already very high. The proportion of total capital accounted for by bank borrowings had tended to rise, especially in Italy and Germany.

There is some statistical evidence for Britain and America to show that this process continued in 1973 and 1974. That would confirm a widespread impression among bankers.

This increase in reliance on fixed-interest borrowing instead of equity meant that even before the oil price went up, the financial system was more vulnerable than in the past. A company under pressure can always pass its dividend; it cannot postpone paying interest on its bank borrowings. So the more highly a company is geared, the more likely it is to be pushed towards defaulting if its profits collapse. After all, failing to pay a dividend means that a company is in difficulties. Failing to pay interest to the bank means that it is bust.

Rising interest rates and contracting money supplies did not just take their toll on the share markets. By spring of 1974, other bubbles were bursting, too. An auction of important Impressionist paintings in London failed to reach the reserve price. Racehorse owners became alarmed by the fall in livestock prices. Above all, the property market was hit.

Property had been a favorite hedge against inflation. In the U.K., where tax relief on mortgages made the cost of home loans relatively cheap, new house prices doubled between 1970 and 1973. Astronomic in Britain, the rise in property values was also large elsewhere. In Germany the average price of developed building land rose by more than a third between 1970 and 1972. In France, in 1968–9, the price of farmland round Paris rose by more than half.

By the first months of 1974 there were signs in some countries—notably Britain and Germany—that property prices were retreating. This threatened the financial system with a new strain. Property companies are more dependent than other companies on asset values for their profits and their balance-sheet totals; and they had tended to employ a system of deficit financing which increased their vulnerability to a collapse of property values.

Thus a property company might buy properties worth $25 million, on which its total return in rents came to only 7 percent. Its interest charges might come to more—say, 10 percent. It would bridge the gap with a conjuring trick, by writing up each year the value of its properties, on the reasonable enough assumption that they were continually increasing in value, and use the written-up value as collateral for still larger loans.

Once property prices started to go down, however, this conjuring trick fell apart. Property companies found that not only could they no longer write up the value of their properties to finance their development—they could hardly sell them. They were hit first by liquidity crises, and then in some cases by bankruptcy. This spread to the banks. In Britain, the "fringe" banks which had lent heavily to property companies ran into serious problems after London and County Securities collapsed in December 1973.

All bankers have one recurrent nightmare: Suddenly all their depositors come in and ask for their money back. Banks carry reserves of spare cash to meet the off-chance that a lot of their customers will take out their money because of some scare. But no bank, however well run, can possibly face the day when every single one of their depositors claim their funds at the same time. Yet this is roughly what happened in the weeks on either side of Christmas 1973 for a host of small and not-so-small London banks. The good suffered with the bad. All it needed was for one rumor, however silly, to go around the market about a bank and that bank would find that they were refused loans on the money markets. A string of banks had to be rescued by their bigger brethren at the behest of the Bank of England. Then some of the rescuers had to be rescued. Then some of the banks that had been rescued once had to be rescued again. As the panic gradually subsided bankers mopped their brows and offered silent thanks to the Bank of England for preventing what might have been the most serious banking crash in British history. A few paused to wonder what might have happened if it had been a foreign bank that had first had this run against it and the Bank of England had not been there. They did not have long to wait.

Sunk on the foreign exchanges

In the first half of 1974, it was stockbrokers who tended to be bankrupted by the collapse of share prices and property companies which tended to be hit by the collapse of property prices. Both put a strain on the banks. But it took losses in the foreign exchange markets to produce banking collapses among large European and American banks.

Throughout 1974 a string of banks revealed some spectacular losses in foreign exchange dealings. With floating exchange rates, it had become much easier for banks to lose at the game of dealing. As long as rates were fixed, a bank only needed to make a one-way bet. Nobody in their right mind would have speculated, in the late 1960s and early 1970s, on a revaluation of the pound, for example. The pound could only be devalued—and the only bank which stood to lose money if that happened was the Bank of England.

But with floating exchange rates, everything became more difficult. Rates might go up as well as down. Sometimes they swung in a single day by more than their entire exchange band under fixed rates. No one knew at what level a central bank might step in and support its exchange rate—nor for how long it would do so.

Foreign exchange dealers worked within limits. In most banks, they are only authorized to hold speculative positions of up to a set amount in each currency. As long as the dealers made money, no one inquired too closely how far they kept to these limits. Then in the course of 1974, a disturbing number of banks began to report that their dealing rooms had run up "unauthorized foreign exchange losses"—"unauthorized," as Christopher Fildes of the London *Evening News* pointed out, "meaning that no one authorized the guys to lose all that money."

Whether it was unauthorized dealing or just plain greed, the list of banks that lost money speculating on foreign exchange reads like a banking *Who's Who.* One of the big three Swiss banks, Union Bank of Switzerland, revealed that while it had been expostulating about the irresponsibility of the British and American authorities in managing their economies, it itself had been busy speculating against sterling and the dollar. One of the German big four, Westdeutsche Landesbank Girozentrale, revealed even heavier losses. (Later came the British Lloyds Bank followed by Banque des Bruxelles in Belgium.)

But these were all big banks, able to lose tens of millions without shaking the security of the bank itself.

Sooner or later, everybody knew, some bank would find that foreign exchange losses had broken it.

In the spring and summer of 1974 it happened to two major banks: in America to the number 20 on the U.S. league, Franklin National Bank, and in Germany to the largest German private bank, I.D. Herstatt of Cologne.

There had already been rumblings of trouble within both the American and German banking systems. A few months earlier banks had been worried by the failure of the National Bank of San Diego, a medium-sized American bank that had done some international business, and by another small German bank. But these had been small fry. Franklin and Herstatt were regarded as sizeable international banks, the sort that no central bank could safely allow to go under.

Franklin was reluctantly propped up. Herstatt was left to go bust.

It was the collapse of Herstatt which did the most damage. It was seriously mishandled by the German monetary authorities. The German credit supervisory board had warned Herstatt the previous April about its excessive foreign exchange operations—but had failed to drive its warning home. Banks in New York were caught in the middle of foreign exchange transactions, because thanks to the transatlantic time difference Herstatt collapsed while the New York foreign exchange market was still open and before some perfectly routine foreign exchange transactions with Herstatt had been completed.

The Herstatt affair proved something of a watershed. It left bankers convinced that it was only a matter of time before other and even more important banks would fail. But worse, it made them fear that they could not expect the world's central banks to bail out any bank that got into difficulties. The next time it happened they might again be on their own.

The failure of Herstatt prompted the central bankers to come to an informal agreement to support banks in liquidity difficulties. But the immediate effect was that the markets seized up. Trading throughout the interconnected markets that make up the international banking system, the foreign exchange market, the Eurodollar market, the international loans market and the various national money markets dropped to a fraction of previous levels. Unfortunately this seizure came just at the time when these markets were being asked to perform new feats . . . to recycle the oil billions.

More than the banks can take

It has been on the commercial banks that the first brunt of recycling has fallen. The first reaction of the oil producers to their newfound wealth has been to put it on deposit with one of the twenty or thirty biggest banks in the world: banks such as Bank of America, Chase Manhattan, First National City Bank, Morgan Guaranty, the big four British banks and a few German and Japanese banks. Normally, Chase or Morgan would be overjoyed by the offer of billions of dollars of deposits. But you can have too much of any good thing . . . and the commercial banks quickly had more oil money than they wanted.

There are, as the banks see it, three problems involved if they are to carry out a large part of the recycling exercise. The first is simple: that the oil producers understandably prefer to lend money for relatively short periods of time. Initially, almost all the oil money was being placed in bank deposits for periods of a week or less. With time this has lengthened. But the potential borrowers who have also been besieging the banks for funds—the countries with deficits—want the money for periods of five, seven or even ten years.

Now, "borrow short and lend long" may be the traditional banker's recipe for disaster. It is also of course how every bank makes its money. But to take in money hand over fist for periods of a week, a month or even six months and to re-lend for a decade involves taking risks that no banker would happily contemplate.

The second problem involved in recycling is the uneven distribution of risk. Any banker would be delighted to do business with the Shah of Iran or even with West Germany: But by the middle of 1974 no banker was interested in lending to Italy, let alone to those unfortunate developing countries whose earnings from the commodity boom had not been enough to sustain their massively increased oil bills. The trouble is, as Chapter 4 argued, that a handful of industrial countries together with the Third World had in 1974 to carry the entire burden of the oil deficit. They are the countries which most desperately need to borrow money. And they were precisely the countries which are the least attractive credit risks.

The third problem is the size of the banks' equity base. A prudent bank keeps an eye on the ratio between its deposits and its equity capital—or if it does not, its central bank certainly does. The difficulty here is the preference of the oil producers for depositing their money with a handful of huge, well-known banks. Within a few months these banks began to worry that their deposits would rise to bigger levels, relative to their capital base, than would be wise. But few banks in 1974 thought of raising more capital. Quite apart from the fact that share prices were depressed and falling, it was clear that recycling was to be a temporary exercise. To dilute existing equity by raising more capital for a strictly temporary exercise would have been hard to explain to shareholders.

Publicly, most central banks in 1974 pooh-poohed these alarms. The total equity capital of the banks in the Eurocurrency market, they reckoned, was quite large enough for them to sustain the whole burden of recycling without raising more capital. But, the banks replied, that ignored the preference of the oil producers for a few large banks. That preference, the central bankers replied, will disappear fast enough once the over-taxed banks begin to cut the rates they offer for deposits. So will the producers' preference for short-term deposits, when the rates for short-term deposits start to fall. Besides (so the central bankers continued) eventually the oil producers will begin to lend directly to borrower countries. Banks may just act as brokers, but they will no longer be prepared to carry huge risks on their books.

As of January 1975, there are some signs that the central banks are partly right. Rates for short-term deposits paid by the biggest banks have begun to be dramatically cut. Oil producers are beginning to explore investments other than bank deposits. But privately the central banks are clearly deeply worried. They saw at the September 1974 meeting of the Bank for International Settlements that they must stand ready to help out any bank in their own countries that ran into foreign exchange difficulties—to act as lenders of last resort to the Eurocurrency markets. But they announced no firm agreement. They left the markets with no clear picture of what types of institution they would underwrite, in what situations they would intervene, and on what terms.

In any event the future of recycling through the Eurocurrency markets must be limited. As Mr. David Rockefeller, Chairman of Chase Manhattan, put it in May 1974: "In general, it is doubtful whether this technique can bridge the gap for more than a year, or at most eighteen months."

Nothing, in the words of the late President Juan Peron of Argentina, has more cowardice than money.

While financial institutions began to lose confidence in each other in 1974, there were no obvious signs of a flight from money. The personal investor still kept his cash in a bank, or a building society, or a pension fund or wherever he had traditionally left it. As long as that happened, there was some hope that worldwide economic collapse would not be accompanied by another Kredit Anstalt. But the stability of any banking system is ultimately dependent on public confidence. One really big bank collapse can destroy that overnight.

Whatever next?

If you are going to be in a car crash, it is better to be wearing safety belts. But it is better still not to be in a crash at all. In the event of a major banking collapse, it is almost unthinkable that the world's central banks would make the same mistakes as they did in the 1930s. Almost certainly they would rally round and support the bank. But how much better to avoid the risk of collapse in the first place!

In January 1975, two vital decisions still faced the international community. They had been identified a full year earlier, at the meeting of the Committee of Twenty in Rome (see Chapter 4) but had still not been dealt with. First, some international machinery was needed to recycle the oil billions, to take some of the strain off the commercial banks. Secondly, some agreement was needed, however rough and ready, on what the share of each country should be in the vast deficit that was the inevitable counterpart of the oil producers' unspendable surplus. Without some such agreement, countries would struggle vainly to return to balance on their international payments—and plunge the world into slump.

Why had no decision been taken before? The answer emerged from the International Monetary Fund's annual meeting in Washington, D.C., at the beginning of October 1974. It was a fundamental difference of view between America and most other industrial countries. The United States still refused to take the problem seriously. American officials took the view that it would not last. Some argued that the oil price, like the price of any other commodity, would fall as demand dropped, and urged policies to conserve fuel; others talked menacingly about the case for military intervention. Others again, more farsighted, pointed out that the oil producers' unspendable surplus revenues would eventually be spent, and that when that day came, it would put an unbearable pressure of extra demand on the resources of the industrial world.

But other countries, notably Britain, took a different view. They argued that the oil price was unlikely to fall by enough to make much difference to the two fundamental decisions that the world had to take. A policy of confrontation with the producers was only likely to strengthen their resolve. The world had to learn to live with the oil money—and had better use it to pay for new investment, in order to have the industrial capacity to meet the producers' demand for goods when it appeared.

But that still left another problem: There was still, by January 1975, no sign whatever of an international agreement on how the oil deficit should be shared out among the rich nations, and between rich and poor. As far as the poor were concerned, a new problem was starting to emerge, quite as intractable as the oil imbalance. It was the problem of food. A few countries, mainly industrial and led by the U.S.A., would produce bigger and bigger surpluses of food over the years ahead. Other countries, among them most of the poorest countries in the world, would find their food production increasingly outstripped by the growth of their population. More and more, they would have to import food in order to eat. They faced a future of mounting food deficits. About this second world imbalance, the internatio al community has only just begun to think.

In the years ahead there are several points at which a dangerous economic situation could become a disastrous one. First—and this is what th book has focused on—the world has to escape from the recession that is now under way without precipitating a yet faster burst of inflation. If all developed countries try to expand their economies simultaneously in 1975–6, they could create a boom more dangerously exaggerated than that of 1972–3. It will not be easy to avoid this as unemployment rises rapidly all over the West in 1975. The U.S.A. has a presidential election coming up in 1976. No government likes to face reelection with too many people out of work.

In early 1975, rising unemployment had frightened a number of governments, including the U.S. administration, into starting to expand their economies. Yet in every major industrial country with the exception of Germany, consumer prices were still rising by 10 percent a year. As the next expansion gathers pace, inflation is sure to accelerate. There is a grave danger —indeed a near certainty—that the boom of 1977–8 will see a number of major countries lose control of their currencies.

There is a second, more immediate danger.

The oil producers may find that the West cannot offer them a safe home for their money and decide that the safest way to protect their savings is to keep their oil in the ground. Alternately, the Arab producers may be tempted to use the oil weapon again in their struggle against Israel. With expensive oil the world might learn to live. Another cut in supplies would be intolerable.

It would be the shortest road *from* the Second Great Crash *to* the Third World War.

APPENDIX: The Other Two Thirds of the World

How the poor got richer

Most of this book has been concerned with the way in which the current world economic crisis affects the rich countries. But for two thirds of mankind, its consequences are much more serious. This appendix deals with the way in which the developing countries—and the rest of the world—are likely to be affected. It begins by explaining that on the eve of the rise in the oil price, many developing countries were doing better than they had ever done before; it ends with a discussion of the looming threat of a world food crisis.

APPENDIX: The Other Two Thirds of the World

Just before the oil price went up, some of the developing countries of the Third World were enjoying a rare lucky break. For fully twenty years, the prices of most commodities and raw materials had been rising more slowly than the prices of manufactured goods. The developing world had had, as the terms of trade moved inexorably against it, to run faster to stay where it was—to export more and more to be able to afford the same amount of imports.

In spite of this, the Third World was managing, by the end of the 1960s, to achieve an average rate of growth that some of the developed countries might have envied. Excluding the oil exporters and China, the total GNP of the Third World grew at an annual average rate of nearly 6 percent between 1968 and 1972, while the industrial countries grew at only 4½ percent.

The growth, of course, was unevenly distributed. Countries like Brazil, Colombia, Korea and Turkey began to emerge as quite prosperous nations, while countries like India, Bangladesh, and some of the Sahelian countries in Africa and some of the Caribbean states were still struggling on the bread line. But it was a hopeful beginning.

Then came the commodity boom of 1972–3. Again, its benefits were not evenly spread. Some countries, such as India, Pakistan and Sri Lanka, found that the commodities which they produced, such as jute and tea, did not share in the general price boom. Others, such as Zaire and Zambia, did extremely well.

Some impression of the overall impact of the commodity price boom on the developing countries can be gained from a glance at their foreign exchange reserves. Leaving the oil exporters aside, developing countries' international reserves rose from less than $15,000 million at the end of 1971 to $27,000 million at the end of 1973 and nearly $31,000 million by April 1974.

Of course, the cost of imports and of servicing the Third World's increasing burden of debt also was rising. But by the end of 1973, at the height of the commodity boom, developing countries were on average undoubtedly better off than they had been five years before. Their gross reserves, at the end of 1973, were the equivalent of about 40 percent of one year's imports and public debt service; five years earlier, in 1968, these had been the equivalent of only about 25 percent.

Although the Third World was having more success in pulling itself up by its own bootstraps in 1972–3, it was getting less assistance from the industrial countries. Official aid was failing to keep pace with the rise in prices. Having boldly committed themselves to the United Nations target of giving 0.75 percent of their GNPs in official aid by 1975, the industrial countries by early 1974 were only managing to give 0.35 percent.

But in the early 1970s, some of the more prosperous Third World countries had found an alternative source of cash—the Eurocurrency market. For those of them with reserves of potentially valuable raw materials, borrowing on the Eurocurrency market offered foreign exchange without all the strings which international agencies and national donors tended to attach. It was expensive—but with commodity prices rising through the roof, who cared?

It so happened that the initial burst of business in the late 1960s that got the medium-term Eurocurrency market off the ground—borrowing by European subsidiaries of mainly U.S. corporations—began to fall away slightly. The banks that ran this market looked around for business and saw not only substantial demand from the Third World, but also that the rise in the price of raw materials had made many of the Third World primary producers perfectly acceptable credit risks.

According to the World Bank, borrowings by less developed countries rose from virtually nothing in 1970, to $3.4 billion in 1972 and $8.2 billion in 1973. That in turn was more than one third of the total Eurocredit volume for 1973 and was approximately double the amount of World Bank group credits to developing countries for the comparable period.

The oil producers turn the screw

Even without the oil price rise, the Third World would probably have had a harder time in 1974 and 1975. There were signs, even before the oil price went up, that the commodity boom was nearing its peak.

Growth in the industrial world was already slowing down. As it did, there would almost certainly have been a fall in commodity prices.

It would probably have been only a moderate fall, and would still have left the prices of most commodities well above their 1971 levels. But with their foreign exchange earnings down, and their markets in the industrial world expanding more slowly, some Third World countries would probably have run into difficulties. The price for the borrowing spree of the previous few years would have had to be paid. The total external public debt of the developing countries, according to the World Bank, was some $55,000 million. Estimates by Pedro-Pablo Kuczynski in *Euromoney* of May 1974 suggest that by the end of 1972 the figure had nearly doubled to $92,000 million, and by 1973 had risen to $105,000 million. Tighter money conditions in 1974 and 1975 would probably have raised the cost of servicing this huge volume of debt in any case.

The oil price rise turned what could have been a difficult couple of years into a dangerous crisis for many developing countries. Saving oil in the rich world may mean turning down a central heating thermostat a few degrees, or flying fewer charter planes. In the Third World it is apt to mean doing without kerosene for cooking and light, or fertilizer and pesticides, or industrial fuel.

Between 1972 and 1973 the developing countries increased their oil imports by a third—from $3,700 million to about $5,000 million. Even if they kept imports at the 1973 level in 1974, the cost of oil to the developing countries was still expected to rise to between $13,000 and $15,000 million.

Indirectly, the oil price rise has hit the Third World in other ways. The $9,000 million or so increase in the cost of oil imports takes no account of the extra cost of oil-derived products, like pesticides and fertilizers. Even before the oil price rise, there was a shortage of oil-based fertilizers. A rise in their price means an additional strain on the balance of payments.

Then, as we have seen, the oil price rise has helped to create the recession in the West. Commodity prices have been badly hit, and the developing countries' main market for their manufactured exports, the industrial world, has contracted sharply.

How badly the balances of payments of Third World countries are affected by the huge rise in the price of imported oil and the slump in the prices of and the demand for their exports is hard to measure. In 1974, it looked as if the trade deficit of the non-oil-exporting developing countries would roughly double, increasing from $11,000 million in 1973 to about $22,000 million.

Once again, not all developing countries suffer equally. All these figures leave aside those developing countries which have actually been made much richer by the oil price rise, because they are members of OPEC. Indeed, six OPEC countries—Algeria, Iran,

Iraq, Indonesia, Nigeria and Venezuela—had run up big debts, both on the Eurocurrency market and to international development agencies when they were rescued by the rise in the oil price. At the end of 1973, their total debts came to $17,000 million, including more than $5,000 million borrowed on the Eurocurrency market since 1970.

There are also several developing countries which do not have enough oil to be notable exporters, but which are on the borders of self-sufficiency. They are countries such as Trinidad, Argentina, Colombia and Peru, and they are partly shielded from the full impact of the OPEC price rise.

But for the rest of the Third World, the price rise has confronted them with a terrible problem. How are they to pay an enormously increased bill?

The poor get poorer

The oil price rise caught the Third World at a time when its reserves were unusually high, and gave it a first line of defense. With reserves at $27,000 million at the end of 1973, it looked as though the average developing country had enough to pay for about four months' of imports at the expected rate for 1974. By letting their reserves fall back to two-and-a-half months' import cover, the Third World could expect to pay for about a third of its deficit.

But again, neither the extra cost of oil nor international reserves was evenly distributed. Some countries, such as Chile and Korea, found themselves caught with a huge increase in their oil bill and relatively low international reserves. Others, such as Sri Lanka and Guyana, had increases in their oil bills that looked small in absolute terms—but again were huge in relation to their tiny international reserves.

At the other end of the scale were Brazil and a few countries like Panama and Thailand, where the oil import bill increased massively in absolute terms but where large reserves made the situation less critical, at least in the short run.

After their reserves, the next line of defense for the better-off developing countries was recourse to the Eurocurrency market. In the first half of 1974, publicly announced medium- and long-term Eurocurrency credits for non-oil-exporting Third World countries came to $4,260 million—little more than $1,000 million less than their entire borrowings in 1973. A few countries—notably the Philippines and Argentina—were actually able to borrow more in the first half of 1974 than in the whole of the previous year.

The high cost of Euromarket borrowings—which is tied to the prevailing interest rates in the Euromarket—has inevitably raised doubts as to the ability of the Third World borrowers to service and repay existing debt. These doubts are all the greater because no mechanism exists to reschedule the Eruomarket debts of countries that find themselves unable to repay. (Official debts can be rescheduled through an informal mechanism known as the Paris Club.) Senior European bankers are naturally concerned that a default by a less developed country could damage the stability of the Western banking system.

But with the industrial countries also struggling to cover their oil deficits, a Third World pauper was bound to find it harder to raise funds in 1974 than in the heyday of the commodity boom. For countries such as India, Pakistan, Sri Lanka, Bangladesh and Sahelian Africa, as well as some of the Caribbean countries which had never had much of a credit rating, Eurocurrency borrowing was virtually out of the question. The main alternative to the Eurocurrency market was aid.

With the industrial countries preoccupied with paying for their own oil bills, 1974 was hardly a good year to ask for more aid. But for the countries in really desperate straits, something like $3,000 to $4,000 million will probably be the very minimum aid that will have to be available before the end of 1975.

Where is it to come from? For first aid, some money might be found simply by diverting aid funds from the twelve major oil exporters. In 1972, these countries were receiving some $770 million, or nearly 10 percent of net aid flows from all OECD sources to the developing world. But at most, probably not more than $2,000 or $3,000 million of this money could easily be redirected.

Another and more promising possibility is for the OPEC countries themselves to give more aid. During 1974, quite a lot was done on a bilateral basis. India worked out what amounted to a two-tier price system with Iran, under which part of the cost of oil imports will be deferred as a debt, and secured one year's credit from Iraq. Pakistan was promised oil at preferential prices by Iran. Several Arab countries, such as Egypt, Syria and Morocco, received direct help from the oil producers.

Plans for OPEC-controlled funds through which loans would be directed from the oil exporters to oil-importing developing countries were also under way. But none of these looked like providing the emergency help for the poorest countries that was clearly going to be needed.

The best hope of that remained in the World Bank. It had already had experience of borrowing from the oil producers: It had placed several bond issues in Kuwait and Libya before the oil price had gone up, and it had also placed a bond issue, denominated in bolivars, in Venezuela. Two questions remained to be resolved, if the World Bank was to recycle funds to the Third World on a big scale. One was the danger of a revaluation by some of the oil producers. The other was the limits imposed by its charter and by its practice on the Bank's ability to carry out general purpose or "program" lending.

Probably an even greater problem than that of organizing emergency aid for the worst hit developing countries will be the problem of coping with a fall in commodity prices. In mid-1974, commodity prices began to fall back from their peaks of spring 1974. But in the first six months of the year, the industrial world's growth decelerated more abruptly than ever before. The deflationary effect of the oil price rise was already probably producing a marked contraction in the world's money supply. Many commodity prices are likely to go on falling throughout 1975.

If this happens, two things are sure. One is that developing commodity producers will try desperately to copy OPEC: to form cartels of their own to stabilize the prices of their main exports. The other is that there will be serious social disruption in some Third World countries.

In the course of 1974, there were already an increasing number of attempts by developing commodity producers to improve their control over prices. Two of the most striking examples were in the production of phosphate and of bauxite, the main raw material for aluminum. In phosphates, no cartel had been set up, but Morocco had used its dominant position to quadruple the price in the year to mid-1974. Other phosphate producers such as Tunisia and Jordan had followed suit.

The main bauxite producers, including Jamaica, Guyana and Surinam, met in Guinea early in 1974 to discuss closer cooperation. Jamaica, which after Australia is the world's biggest bauxite producer and which has the added advantage of being close to the vital U.S. market, unilaterally increased revenue payments by the aluminum companies eightfold. Attempts to follow the Jamaican example quickly were made by the smaller bauxite producers of Guyana and the Dominican Republic.

In May, the six producers of mercury agreed to try to raise prices by 20 to 30 percent. In March, some of the main iron ore producers agreed to form a cartel. Thirteen tea exporters got together and decided to cut the export quota for the 1974–5 tea crop by 23,000 tons, to try to keep prices up by enough to recoup the increased cost of fertilizer. The rubber producers met and decided to set up a buffer stock to stabilize prices.

In mid-November 1974 came what could be the most important attempt of all. The world's main copper exporters—Peru, Chile, Zambia and Zaire—met in Paris and decided to cut their exports by 10 percent from the beginning of December, in an attempt to halt the collapse of the copper price, which had more than halved since the summer of 1973. The copper producers' club, CIPEC, is responsible for something under 40 percent of all world production of copper—as OPEC is for oil. But where OPEC controls about 90 percent of world exports of oil, CIPEC controls under 70 percent of world exports of copper. And 40 percent of all copper used is recycled scrap. Finally, the CIPEC countries lack the religious and political bonds which have helped to hold OPEC together.

Probably not even the copper producers will have a major impact on prices. In all these schemes, either the producers are too numerous, or they lack the political drive of the OPEC countries, or their cartels do not include some important developed producer of raw materials. But some of them may well help to keep commodity prices above the levels to which they would otherwise fall.

If, in spite of the efforts of the producers, there is a collapse of commodity prices, then the gravest danger for the industrial world will be the currents of political unrest that will be set in motion. The Third World needs growth and rising real incomes to ensure stability even more than the industrial world. There is probably much more danger of a collapse of the government of a major developing country—say India or Brazil—under the strain of a world slump than of a coup or revolution in one of the richer countries of the West.

The world food crisis

To the problems of many Third World countries was added in late 1974 a further worry. This was that the world grain harvest looked no better than mediocre. With cereal stocks already run down by the disastrous harvest of 1971–2, that meant a real food shortage for some of the larger food importers, and for all, the worrying prospect of a further rise in the price of grain.

Looking further ahead, the food problem appears increasingly intransigent. Food production in the developing countries has been growing rapidly for more than a decade—just as fast, indeed, as in the richer countries. But population in the Third World has been growing faster still. Before the Second World War, the developing countries as a group had been net exporters of cereals. By the end of the 1960s, only Argentina, Burma, Mexico and Thailand were large exporters of cereals. By the second half of the 1960s, the developed countries were the world's main exporters of cereals, providing two thirds of the total, with the United States alone providing half.

Looking ahead, the developing countries are likely to need to import foodstuffs on a larger and larger scale. One estimate, by the United Nations, suggests that by 1985 they will need to import 85 million tons a year in a normal year—and 100 million tons in a year of drought or flood. The developed countries may have a large enough surplus of food to fill this need. But how are the developing countries to pay for their food? Will the rich food exporters try to impose ever more stringent terms in return for feeding the rest of the world? If the mid-1970s have seen the world dominated by the politics of oil, the end of this decade will surely see it dominated by the politics of food.